The Positivity Project

Marie Parkinson

The Positivity Project

Copyright © Marie Parkinson, 2024

First published in 2024 by Marie Parkinson

ISBN [Insert number]

Edited and typeset by Carl Mynott & Marie Parkinson

Cover design by Carl Mynott & Marie Parkinson

The rights of Marie Parkinson to be identified as the author of this work has been asserted in accordance with the Copyright, Designs and Patents Act, 1988. All rights reserved. No part of this publication may be reproduced, stored in a retrieval system, or transmitted, in any form or by any means (electronic, mechanical, photocopying, recording or otherwise), without the prior written permission of the publisher. This book is sold under the express understanding that any decisions or actions you take as a result of reading this book must be based on your judgement and will be at your sole risk. The author will not be held responsible for the consequences of any actions and/or decisions taken as a result of any information given or recommendations made.

A CIP catalogue record for this book is available from the British Library.

Printed and bound by Amazon KDP

For Aileen

who calls me her human rainbow,
and whose own sunlight makes the world a better place.

Acknowledgements

I'd like to express my gratitude to the lovely people who shared their time and energy with me during our original social media projects, especially Paula who requested that we do it all a second time. Thank you for triggering a chain of events that has led me to spend this time in soulful solitude, creating something which has given me a strong sense of purpose and satisfaction.

Thank you to Laura whose warm heart and beautifully coloured guest room provided me with the space I needed to be creative, inspired and intuitively guided to write this book. Thank you for participating in the projects too, your input has always been valuable.

Thank to my soul brother, Carl, who has not only encouraged and held me accountable from the start, but also taken the time and trouble to edit my work. Thank you for being a part of and participating in the projects, and for your never-ending support. You, my friend, are a fellow positivity powerhouse indeed!

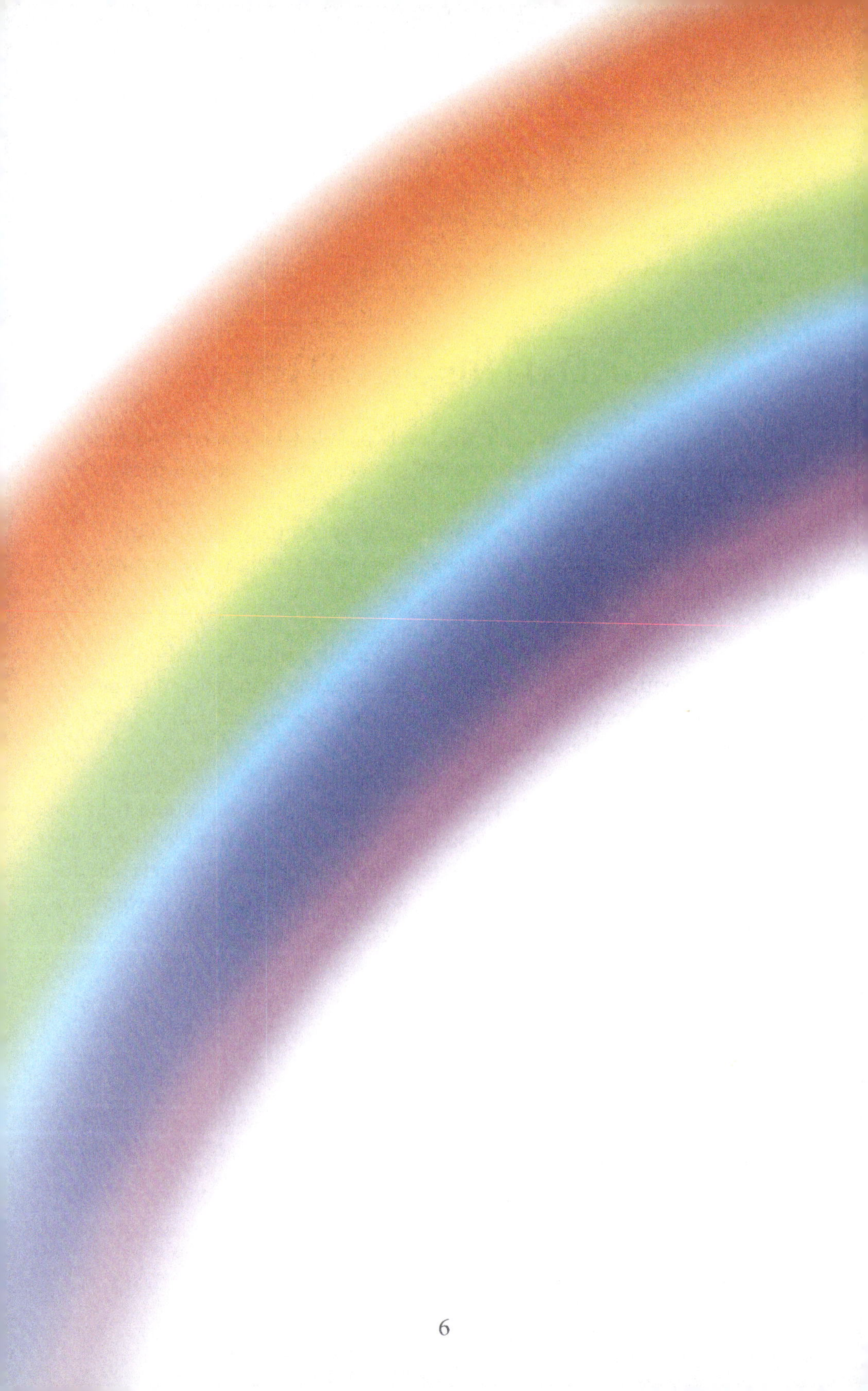

Contents

Acknowledgements	5
Introduction	9
Gratitude	11
Nature	19
Exercise	33
Nutrition	41
Self-love	49
Setting boundaries	57
Positive influences	67
Generosity	73
Colour	81
Affirmation	103
Meditation	111
Release	121
Finding Joy	129
Play!	135
Conclusion	141

"Why are you so positive all the time?"

"How are you so positive all the time?"

"You're the most positive person I know. How do you that?"

"You're too positive, it's really annoying."

"I love your positivity, it's uplifting to be around."

Introduction

Whether they love it or not, my positive energy is the one thing about me that people have always commented on the most. These types of comments and questions are what led me to create a social media project in the lockdown of November 2020, called 'The Positivity Project'. Rather than finding a single way to answer the question "How are you so positive all the time?", I thought it would be better to actually show people, inviting them to try a few of the methods I have learned and incorporated into my own life for themselves.

The following 14 "positivity practices", as I have come to call them, are practical ways in which we can all improve our mindset and enhance our personal wellbeing. They are all relatively straightforward, readily available, effective and, for the most part, free! Each of them is an invitation to create new and healthier habits for ourselves, and they can help us to cultivate an enduring, positive attitude.

Many of those who took part in the original 14-day project, said they enjoyed it and found it valuable. It was when I had a request from one of them in the summer of 2021 to do it all again that I reworked the project into a more fun and interactive, 7-day series. That's when I realised that there's so much more value that I could offer on each subject, and so the idea for this book had germinated.

My aim is for the guidance, tools, and techniques described on the following pages to be of value and service to others.

I invite you to peruse each subject at your own leisure, and to try any or all of the activities I have recommended for yourself. If you find something which really resonates with you, you are welcome to take it on board. If you find which something doesn't suit you, I would suggest that you simply disregard it. That which works well for some of us just might not be another's cup of tea. It is down to you to decide for yourself which positivity practices you would like to bring into your daily life, and it is for you to find the most appropriate way in which you can incorporate them.

Gratitude

Grow your gratitude with a daily practice.

Gratitude is, in my opinion, the foundation of a positive mindset. It's my first and most fundamental positivity practice - if you choose to adopt just one of my recommendations, I would strongly suggest that you make it this one. When it comes to gratitude, the good news is that, not only is it one of the most beneficial, it's also one of the simplest and quickest ways to establish a more positive mindset.

No matter how rotten we feel, focusing on things for which we can be grateful can swiftly shift our perspective away from the negative, gently uplifting our mood at the same time. It's something which is very easy to do and can be practiced anywhere and at any given moment. Practicing gratitude when we are already feeling good serves to elevate us further, creating a springboard which can catapult us to new heights and building appreciation and resilience along the way. It might help to think of gratitude as the launchpad of our rocket, sending us up to a healthier and happier version of ourselves in our minds, bodies, and in our souls.

Studies in neuroscience show that on a chemical level, the brain is positively impacted during gratitude practice, producing the feel-good hormones, dopamine and serotonin. It's a valuable tool which literally rewires the brain to make us feel happier and more motivated. Practicing gratitude on a daily basis will improve feelings of self-worth and compassion, as well as reducing stress, depression, and anxiety. It can also help to reduce physical pain and improve the function of our immune systems. With so many benefits, it's difficult to find a reason not to practice gratitude.

So, how does it work? Well, we simply take a moment to pause and think of things that we are grateful for. Such things might include people, places, things, and situations. We can either say them out loud, think of them quietly in our own minds, or we can write them down. Some people keep a gratitude journal in which they write down things for which they are grateful every day. A gratitude journal can serve as a helpful reminder when we're having a bad day and need something positive to look back on.
I personally practice gratitude by simply asking myself every day, "What five things am I grateful for today?" and I make a point of saying them out

loud. I frequently do this whilst I'm out walking my dog, but I don't always remember to do this. Because of this, I have set a daily reminder on my phone which goes off at 9pm each evening.

When it comes to thinking of things for which you can be grateful, it might not seem so simple initially, particularly if we are feeling low. A great place to start is by focusing on those people in our lives who love us; family, friends, colleagues, or even our pets! Starting here helps us to consciously appreciate those people and directly contributes to an increase in our own happiness. Perhaps there has been a positive interaction in your day which you can be thankful for. Something as simple as a smile or a "Good morning!" from a neighbour, or even from a stranger in the street.

Let's think about your surroundings? You might appreciate the view from your window, or that lovely place where you walk your dog. It could be a beautiful sunrise or the smell of your favourite fragrance. Some days it's easy to find happy or extraordinary things to be grateful for, but there are days where this can be tougher, and we may need to dig a little deeper. Every one of us has bad days from time to time, and we all experience stress at some point in our lives - these are the times when it's most helpful for us to look for the simplest and most basic of things for which we can be grateful. Fundamental things such as the shelter of our homes, the clean water that we drink, and the food on our plates which nourishes us. It also helps us to not take these things for granted. Being grateful for all the people who have played a part in making it possible for us to support these basic needs, takes it to another level. Think about the farmers who grow and harvest our food, the delivery person who transports it to the shop where you bought it, the supermarket staff who unpack and sell it, and so on. Taking gratitude to this deeper level shifts our perspective and boosts our mood, even on tough days. When we practice gratitude, we begin to feel calmer, less isolated and more optimistic. It can help to cultivate feelings of contentment and bring more peace into our lives.

The law of attraction tells us that by focussing on what we already have and being thankful for it, will naturally attract more things into our lives to be thankful for. So, there's another reason to bring this healthy habit into your life - starting right now!

As with any skill, long-term practice is the key to establishing consistent results. I invite you to try to incorporate a gratitude practice into your daily routine for 30 days, paying close attention to your mindset as it begins to shift for the better.

Positivity in practice

Throughout this book I have included practical activities to help you incorporate positivity practices into your regular routines. For example, I might suggest you ask yourself "Which 5 things am I grateful for today?" and either speak each of them out loud, or quietly in your own mind as you answer. The first of these collections of activities is presented to you below, and they relate to the practicing of gratitude...

Cultivate a daily gratitude practice

Set a daily reminder on your device, with a cheerful tone or song. Choose any time that suits you. When the reminder sounds off each day, express 3-5 things that you feel grateful for.

Create a gratitude journal

Some people prefer to write things down. This might be so that they can look back and reflect upon them at a later date, or simply to help cement something into their minds. If this approach appeals to you, I suggest that choose a new notebook and maybe even a brand-new pen and begin a daily gratitude journal.

Create a visual reminder

Write a reminder or an affirmation on a sticky-note or postcard, and leave it somewhere that you will see it regularly. You could incorporate a reminder in the screensaver or lock screen on your device. You can create your own or use one of these suggestions:

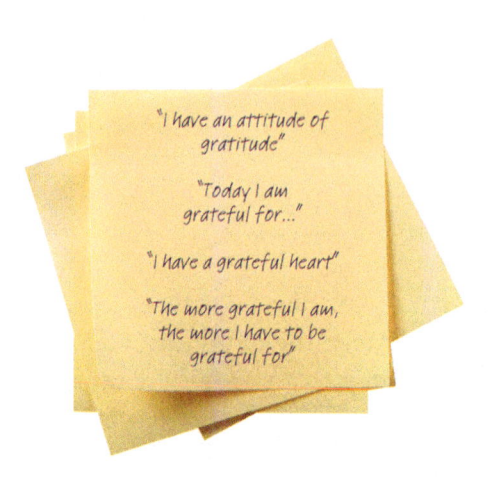

"I have an attitude of gratitude"

"Today I am grateful for..."

"I have a grateful heart"

"The more grateful I am, the more I have to be grateful for"

Speak your reminder or affirmation out loud. Try to invoke feelings of gratitude, and maybe even smile as you say it.

Express gratitude to someone else

Contact someone you know and express your gratitude towards them - let them know why you are grateful for them. You could call them, or send them a written note, text or email. Sending written expressions of gratitude is great because they can keep it to look back on.

Incorporate colour into your gratitude practice

Use the colour green to enhance your practice. Green stationery would be ideal!

Grow your Gratitude

What are you grateful for today?

Strengths
Resilience
Patience
Ability to Overcome
Challenges

Small things
Things that Made You
Laugh/Smile
Sunshine
Yoga Class

Roots/Foundations
Your Home
Family/Friends
Basic Needs (shelter/water)
Your Body

Nature

Nourish yourself with Mother Earth.

Having already established that gratitude forms the foundation of uplifting my mindset and mood, I will now go on to add that Nature is my life's setting, or backdrop.

Spending time in nature is incredibly beneficial for us on all levels; physical, mental, emotional, and spiritual. It's one of **the** best things we can do for ourselves. Whether I'm walking, wild-swimming, gardening, watching the sunset, moon-gazing, or simply having a cup of tea in my garden, being in nature always makes me feel connected, grounded, and renewed. It has a very calming and restorative effect.

Many of us find the effects of a tiring day at work can be soothed away by taking a walk in nature, even if it's just a short walk and is taken at a gentle pace. There's something naturally medicinal about breathing fresh air into our lungs, feeling the warmth of sunshine on our skin, and letting the wind blow away any mental or emotional cobwebs. Quite often it seems to be most beneficial when we start out thinking that we can't be bothered to go outside - these are the times when we come back inside feeling the most refreshed.

I like to think of spending time outdoors as like getting a hug from Mother Nature. She can be a wonderful companion and a nourishing supporter in times of stress and anxiety, especially when we find ourselves experiencing feelings such as fear, confusion, uncertainty, loneliness, or isolation.

Being among ancient woodlands and rivers can really help to shift our perspective; focusing on the knowledge that the trees, rocks and rivers have been there since long before we were born - and will most likely be there long after we're gone - can give us a sense of feeling that we are but a small part of something much bigger than ourselves. This can then help us to reduce the intensity of our own worries and stresses. They somehow seem to shrink and feel less significant, swiftly shifting our mood for the better and providing us with a sense of optimism, connection and clarity. If there's a decision that needs to be made or a problem that needs solving, I would recommend taking a little break outside first. It does us the world of good to pause and (literally) get outside of our own heads.

Observing the plants and animals in nature, we can see how they naturally respond to the cycles of the changing seasons; here in the northern hemisphere trees know when to begin new growth in spring, when to bloom in summer, when to shed their leaves in autumn, and when to become dormant during the winter months before repeating it all again the following year. Hibernating animals intuitively know when to reawaken and become active during spring & summer, feeding their young families, and finding new homes. They sense when it is time to to fill their bellies or food stores during autumn, in order to prepare for the winter months. Instinctively following these patterns ensures their growth and survival enabling them to take care of their health needs along the way.

Just as the trees and animals know when to grow, bloom, release, and hibernate, we too can take inspiration from their example; every season has its own purpose. This ancient wisdom teaches us to trust that all things are temporary and will unfold at their own pace. Nature doesn't try to force or rush the process, so why should we? Let's allow it to inspire and guide us, just like our ancestors once did. It can be of great benefit to us if we can learn to surrender a little more and go with the natural flow of life…

Living in alignment with the rhythms of nature.

The most frequent and natural cycle is the circadian rhythm, which is also known as the cycle of day and night, light and dark. Our bodies instinctively know how to be awake and more alert during daylight hours, just as they also know it's time to go to sleep when it gets dark. This rhythm is considered to be both healthy and natural, with most of us physically responding well to it. Paying attention to this natural cycle can benefit us all, but especially those who suffer from seasonal affective disorder (SAD). Ensuring we spend some time outdoors in the daylight can help to support us through the darker months of the year. During the winter, many of us rarely see daylight at home because we are leaving for work in the dark mornings and arriving home after dark in the evenings. If possible, it's wise to go outside into the daylight during our break at work, even if the weather is cold. On days off, it's worth spending longer periods of time in daylight. Sunlight is known to uplift our mood and improve our ability to focus, as well as helping the body to produce vitamin D. It also strengthens our immune systems and reduces fatigue. If going outside isn't an option, being in a room which is naturally well-lit is a good substitute. We can use nature to help us overcome the winter blues by opening the curtains and blinds, letting the light in, and positioning ourselves so that we can, at the very least, see outside.

It's worth noting the negative impact that working night shifts or variable shift patterns can have on our health. Research shows that they can increase the risk of heart attacks, obesity, depression, anxiety, premature ageing, and memory loss (dementia), among other things. The list goes on. It's estimated that 10-40% of shift workers suffer from shift-work sleep disorder (SWSD). Whilst for financial reasons it can be a necessity to work shifts, it's well known to be better for our health and well-being to work during daytime hours - in alignment with the circadian rhythm. Making the effort to consciously connect with nature can be hugely beneficial for shift workers.

Our ancient ancestors understood the benefits of being guided by the rhythms of nature, following the seasons of the earth and the patterns occurring in the skies. While our current calendar is based upon the cycle of earth's orbit around the sun, before Roman times many civilisations followed the cycles of the moon and used them as a guide. Farmers would plant, grow, and harvest their crops in alignment with the lunar phases, enabling them to improve the success rate and quality of their produce, but more importantly ensuring their survival.

While it's common knowledge that the moon's gravitational pull affects the tidal ebb and flow of the oceans, the impact it can have on us humans is often overlooked. Our physical bodies are made up of approximately 60% water - which includes our brain fluid, so it makes sense that this natural force influences our mental and emotional well-being.

Paying attention to the lunar cycles, particularly the main eight phases of the moon, and making appropriate lifestyle changes, can help us to live a more balanced, healthier, and happier life.

Moon phase guide

There are 13 lunar cycles in a year, each lasting approximately 29.5 days. Each cycle can be divided into 8 main phases, with each having its own energetic influence which affects the earth itself, as well as the living things on it. Generally speaking, the first half of the moon cycle is an increasing energy, while the second half is a decreasing energy - much like the ebb and flow of an ocean's tide.

Over the next few pages, I'll explain each moon phase in a little more detail to help you align your own lifestyle to suit the moon's relative phases.

New Moon

This is the time to set new intentions and plant the seeds of new growth. However, in order to welcome in the new, it's important to clear out the old first. The new moon is a great time to mentally and emotionally let go of anything which no longer serves us. It's like wiping the slate clean so that we can write a new chapter of our lives. Centuries ago, women would gather in groups to hold space and support each other around the time of a new moon, an ancient tradition that is making a welcome comeback in modern times.

Waxing Crescent

As the first slivers of the moon begin to appear in the skies once again, this symbolises a growing energy. We begin to feel an increase in motivation and physicality. This moon phase encourages us to actively start new projects, or to gently breathe fresh life back into ongoing ones.

First Quarter

During this phase the moon is half visible, and half in darkness as she continues her orbit around the earth. It's a time when we can really get going; taking inspired action based upon the intentions we set at the new moon. Making lists and checking them off daily is a good way to align with this energy, it'll help us to achieve our goals. Sometimes we may feel pulled in opposing directions at this time, so if necessary, it's wise to take a moment to pause and reevaluate here. It's ok to change our minds and discard anything which isn't feeling in alignment, especially if we've perhaps been over-ambitious in setting ourselves impossible tasks. Now is the time to focus on what is achievable and to move forward with that in mind.

Waxing Gibbous

As the moon appears to grow, illuminating more than half of her surface in the light of the sun, our energy increases too! The days leading up to a full moon can feel quite intense and even anxious at times, this increase in energy can be utilised for creativity and productivity, helping us to get things done. It's wise to be mindfully aware of our thoughts and feelings at this time as the incoming full moon energy will highlight anything within us that is calling to be drawn out and healed.

Full Moon

An exciting time when the moon is shining brightly and can be fully seen - and it reminds us that we should be too! It's an empowering time which boosts our confidence and motivation. Now is the time to complete projects and reap the rewards of our harvest, so to speak. The full moon energy is potent and powerful, like a high tide and is another good time to gather with friends to hold sacred space for each other (or simply by ourselves). It can be used to once again release and let go of anything that no longer serves us, particularly anything that has arisen since the new moon. It's also a 'magnetic' time that invites us to manifest anything we need, seek to have more of, or to attract into our lives.

Waning Gibbous

The days after a full moon are a joyous time to celebrate and give thanks for all the good in our lives. It's a great time to socialise and simply enjoy spending time with the people we love. It's also a good time to break bad habits, so if there's anything we'd like to give up or 'push away', attuning to the energy of a waning moon will help us to be more successful. As the earth's shadow begins to expand across the moon's surface as she wanes, she will reflect less light and appear to get smaller and smaller each day/night now and our physical energy will begin to slow down.

Last Quarter

As the moon is once again exactly half in darkness and half in light, this phase offers us a chance to release; it's beneficial to de-clutter and reorganise our homes and even our workspaces at this time. It's also a wonderful energy to use to practice forgiveness, allowing anything that's been weighing you down to be released, like the tide of an ocean as it ebbs away from the shore.

Waning Crescent

Also known as the "dark moon" phase. This when the moon appears to slip more and more into darkness before 'disappearing' fully as the new moon approaches. This is when we tend to feel the most physically tired and often emotionally drained, often likened to an ocean's low tide. Feeling withdrawn, fed up or empty around this time is common, and it's a natural invitation for us to take a well-earned rest. The energy of this moon is a fantastic time to focus on retreating, relaxing and restoring. Now is the time to simply surrender and to trust that the universe is conspiring in our favour.

Earthing

Nature really is the best medicine, and Mother Earth is abundant with healing energy.

"Earthing" is a therapeutic technique where positively charged electrons from the earth's energy field - known as negative ions - are transferred into the human body, promoting natural healing, and restoring functions. It can improve physical health such as boosting immunity, whilst reducing inflammation, pain, and fatigue. It also has mental and emotional benefits that include reducing anxiety and depression.

Methods include connecting to the Earth with the soles of our feet - an entry point on the body where negative ions are easily absorbed. It is said that spending 10 minutes barefoot on the earth each day can boost our immune systems. The palms of our hands are the same, which is why getting stuck into soil and touching plants when gardening can give us that feel-good factor! Laying on the ground, leaning with our back against a tree, and wild swimming are also great ways of earthing. Cold-water exposure is known to build resilience both physically and mentally, strengthening our immune and cardiovascular systems - it's great fun, feels amazing and it's free too! No wonder it's becoming so popular these days.

High quantities of negative ions are emitted by flowing water, which is why being near streams, rivers, and waterfalls can make us feel so good. When rain hits the ground, it emits a certain fresh and uplifting smell, known as 'petrichor'. When this occurs, negative ions are released, literally making us feel happy. A "pluviophile"- is a word which is used to describe a lover of rain; someone who finds joy and peace of mind on rainy days. I love this - I am definitely a pluviophile! I relish rainy days and thoroughly enjoy the sounds of rain on my windows, roof, and even on my umbrella.

It's not always possible or practical to spend as much time as we would like outside. Life and its constant demands can get in the way, and physical limitations might be a restricting factor for some people. This is where it's valuable to understand that we can invite nature to come to us - by bringing the outdoors, inside...

Hygge

Hygge (pronounced Hoo-gah) is a Danish word that doesn't have a direct English translation. The best way to describe it, is as a way of life or well-being. It's more of a feeling, rather than something you can buy and themes associated with it are gratitude, mindfulness, security/comfort, social connections, and nature.

While spending quality time outside in nature is conducive to a hygge lifestyle, for the purpose of incorporating it into the positivity practices that can improve our wellbeing, let's focus on how we can bring nature in to our homes and workspaces.

The Danes and their Scandinavian neighbours understand and appreciate the importance of well-lit spaces; letting in as much natural light as possible is really healthy for us. Something as simple as opening the windows and allowing fresh air to circulate can boost our immune systems, reduce symptoms of anxiety and depression, and help us to sleep better.

Fireplaces and candles are a source of natural light (and warmth), and therefore using them has an uplifting effect on our mood, as well as providing us with a sense of coziness and comfort. They are especially supportive during dark evenings and throughout the winter months.

Incorporating nature into our living spaces is considered to be very hyggelig (nice, pleasant), and is known to have a calming effect on us. Introducing houseplants is a good way to start, because they purify the air we breathe, reducing toxins, and increasing oxygen in the room. Having them in the bedroom can help us to sleep better. Taking care of them can also bring us feelings of satisfaction and a sense of purpose, which in turn reduces stress and can help to alleviate mild depression. So, whether you're an outdoor or indoor gardener, well-experienced, or a complete novice, the mental health benefits of connecting to nature in this way, are available to us all.

Adding elements of nature to our decor is a particularly effective way in which we can bring the outdoors inside; images of plants, flowers, landscape views, and wildlife are easily accessible, and they can provide splashes of cheerful colour which help to uplift our mood. They can even help to boost creativity.

Himalayan salt lamps make excellent decor within the home because not only do they give off a soft, cozy glow but they also purify air and emit mood-boosting negative ions. Having one in the room with you is definitely a positive thing!

Foraging for, and arranging, our own natural decor such as flowers, seashells, and things like pine cones is both fun and free. We can display them in any way we choose, or even use them to make our own decorations - handmade gifts are very hyggelig too!

Aromatherapy is another way in which we can enhance our indoor environments; many people find the smell of fresh flowers to be uplifting. Scented candles, wax melts, and oil burners not only freshen the smell of a room, but they can also have a positive effect on our psychology too. Essential oils in particular, are very beneficial for both soothing or uplifting, balancing and restoring our moods and emotions. They can also be used as a holistic or complementary therapy to improve our physical health too, often being added to bath water or massage oils.

So, as you can see, nature is a gift that we can connect to in body, mind, and spirit. I invite you to allow it to inspire you and to find some ways in which it can support your health, happiness and well-being.

Positivity in practice

Spend some quality time outdoors

Whether it's exercising, gardening or sitting beside a window, put away your devices for a chosen duration of time and really pay attention to the sights, sounds and smells of nature around you

Stand or walk barefoot on the earth

Collect or forage something from nature;

This could be pine cones, leaves, flowers, fruit, sand, sea glass or shells.. display your gifts from nature in your home or workspace.

Watch a sunrise or sunset, either alone or with loved ones.

Spend some time star gazing and moon bathing on a clear night.

Have an outdoor picnic.

Incorporate nature into your interior decor

This could be a picture, a textile design for soft furnishings or bringing in a houseplant.

Stream a nature inspired, ambient video on YouTube

Exercise

Move your body, shift your mindset.

We all know that exercise is good for the body, but what we often forget is that it's also one of the best ways to uplift our mood and support a healthy mindset. Experiencing stress and anxiety is a natural part of human life, all of us have these experiences and there's nothing we can do to stop it from happening.

There are many ways in which we can support ourselves through it though, and one of the best ways to combat stress is with exercise. When we exercise, we produce those much-loved feel-good hormones such as endorphins, dopamine, oxytocin, and serotonin.

Endorphins

Releasing endorphins can relieve pain, reduce stress and produce feelings of euphoria.

Dopamine

Dopamine is a 'feel-good' and 'reward' hormone which is responsible for allowing you to feel pleasure, satisfaction and motivation.

Oxytocin

This is the 'cuddle hormone' which reduces blood pressure and levels of cortisol, promotes growth and healing, regulates emotional responses

Serotonin

This hormone stabilises our mood and helps to regulate our sleep.

All of these "happy hormones" are naturally produced during exercise and are known to help improve our mood, as well as reducing anxiety and depression. For those of us who were never sporty kids at school, who lack confidence, or suffer from social anxiety, it can be daunting to start showing up at fitness classes or to find the courage to join a gym. Let me reassure you though, that if this resonates with you, you are not alone! I believe that all of us have the capability to find a form of exercise which will suit our needs and circumstances, it might just require a little bit of an adventurous spirit to discover it.

I was one of those kids at school who hated sports. I didn't know what 'social anxiety' was back then, but I knew I felt awkward and uncomfortable taking part in group activities and struggled with cardio-based exercise because I was asthmatic. I would dread sports days because I felt inadequate and embarrassed, and would find any excuse I could to get out of taking part in them! (It's also worth noting that at that time that didn't know what an "introvert" was - it wasn't until I was in my early thirties that the penny dropped on that one!).

It was when I finished college and stopped partying that I discovered yoga, and eventually fell in love with exercising. The difference being that it was now my choice to do it - I was no longer cringing at being forced into physical action by seemingly unsympathetic school teachers. Now I was actually exercising because I wanted to. I was having fun and it made me feel good.

Yoga eased my aching body after a tiring day at work and lifted my spirits when I felt low. After the devastating and life-changing loss of my dad to a sudden heart attack when I was 14, I spent my teenage years under a dark cloud of depression. Not knowing how to navigate the murky waters of grief, which I hid well beneath a brave face and without any professional help or support, I had to somehow find my own way out of it. I credit my yoga practice with starting my healing process - I'd found something I actually enjoyed and looked forward to doing. I met lovely, like-minded people in the classes I tried and through my practice, I somehow seemed to magically release the emotional blockages I'd been stuck with for far too long. I discovered that yoga is so much more than exercise, I no longer felt mentally weighed-down and this outlet for emotional release helped me to begin to feel free.

If left untended, emotions can become stuck and this can cause problems within the physical body. Anything which doesn't have an outlet of release can become suppressed and subsequently problematic, manifesting as aches, pains, tightness, and tiredness. Any dis-ease within the mind can turn into disease within the body, which is why exercising is such a valuable tool for releasing tension and stress.

It turns out that yoga is an ideal form of exercise for those of us who have introverted personalities. Being on the yoga mat enables us to spend quality time on our own (even when we're in a class full of people), and it's certainly where I feel most 'at home' with myself. It's not for everyone though and there plenty of other types of exercise for us to try, both on our own and with other people. Any kind of exercise is beneficial for us, and it can be really helpful to share the experience with a friend, especially when trying something or somewhere new for the first time. It can also help us to feel inspired, motivated, connected, and supported. Exercising with others helps to keep us on track, aiding us to achieve our goals - you can't beat a bit of friendly encouragement (or competition if that's what works for you!).

For this positivity practice, I recommend creating a daily or weekly routine to make it more effective because consistency is key. Having a regular time for exercise helps us integrate it into our lives and make it a healthy habit that we can stick to. Choosing a variety of activities is wise because, not only will it prevent us getting bored, but each type of exercise will have different health benefits for our physical bodies.

I like to exercise first thing in the morning as part of my daily routine, and my main reason for doing so is for the benefit of my mental health - it helps to dissolve any anxiety that I may have woken up with and it sets me up nicely for the day ahead. Sometimes I might only practice yoga for 10-15 minutes, but a little something is better than nothing at all. As long as we're moving our body and having fun, we're going to reap the rewards of our efforts, both mentally and physically.

Mornings may not suit everyone, and so an evening routine might work better. The "two-minute rule" is a great way to ensure we don't skip an exercise session; literally get changed as soon as you get home from work and either start exercising within two minutes, or be out the door before we get distracted or delayed. The feel-good after effect is great motivation; the satisfaction of achievement far outweighs the feelings of disappointment that we would have if we didn't show up for ourselves.

As well as reducing stress, anxiety and depression, exercise has many other benefits including improved concentration, memory, self-confidence, and self-worth. Aiding in clear thinking and decision making. Boosting energy levels, balancing hormones, and supporting cognitive function. We also sleep better when we exercise regularly, which is a major contributing factor to our happiness.

All of these beneficial factors make exercise high on my priority list and for that reason, it's one of the top tools that I can recommend for improving our well-being and cultivating a positivity mindset.

Positivity in practice

If you already have a well-established exercise routine, give thanks for your body and your efforts, and keep up the good work!

Try something new

If you're currently not very active, try starting small such as a ten-minute walk around the block, or a gentle exercise video on you tube.

Try something different

Switch up your routine by trying a different type of exercise, or walking/running a new route.

Set a goal

This could be to exercise consistently for a set number of days, or to increase your activity time. Choose any new goal that is realistic and achievable, and get to it. Writing down our goals will improve our success rate.

Buddy up

Goals are more likely to be achieved if you have someone or something to hold you accountable. Ask a friend to either join you in your exercise or pursuit of a shared goal, or ask them if you can report your activities to them as you go.

Track your progress

There are many free apps to help you track your progress, many of which connect you to friends or others within your community. Perhaps explore what's available online and download one that resonates with you.

Nutrition

You are what you eat...

The food we choose to put in our body not only affects our physical health but also has a big impact on our mental well-being too! Let me be completely honest – I am not an expert on the subject of nutrition, and it's actually my Achilles heel when it comes to my own positivity practices. This is why I feel it's really important for me to not give up on this one, and to keep striving to practice and improve my choices when it comes to nutrition.

You may have heard the phrases "you are what you eat" and "mood food". Let's take a closer look at what they mean, and how we can use this information to make improvements to our health, mindset, and overall well-being…

Essentially, the foods we consume are our body's fuel. Just like a car, the quality of the fuel we put in will influence the overall performance of the machine. If we fill our tanks with unhealthy fuels like junk food and stimulants such as caffeine, sweeteners, and alcohol, the body will not perform as optimally as it could. If instead, we choose to consume healthy and clean foods, such as vegetables, proteins, minerals, and vitamin-rich foods, the body will be able to function and perform at a higher level.

There's a good reason why athletes and sports people eat a healthy diet - they want to perform to the best of their ability, and they understand the importance of how their diet can help them to do it, both physically and mentally.

The body and mind are interlinked, and the foods we eat have a direct impact on the way in which the mind functions. Essentially, junk food = junk mood, while good food = good mood!

Now this doesn't mean we should never indulge in a little bit of the sweet stuff - a few treats won't do us any long-lasting harm. Quitting every 'unhealthy' food we enjoy, or completely overhauling our diet, is highly unrealistic and certainly not sustainable. It's like my grandmother always told me - and I love this - "everything in moderation". It's all about finding a balance!

Being mindful of the foods we eat and how they make us feel is something that we need to become consciously aware of if we want to support our mental health and wellbeing. From that point of awareness, we can then decide if and what small changes we would like to make in order to help us move forward in a positive direction.

I've always had a really sweet tooth (and unfortunately, I have the fillings to prove it), but there's a big difference between how I feel when I'm regularly eating cakes, sweets and biscuits, compared to when I choose to stay off them for a while. When I cut out refined sugar from my diet, I always feel happier, mentally calmer, and more physically energetic. I find that I become more motivated and generally less stressed!

When I choose healthier options, such as snacking on fruit and adding more vegetables to my meals, I start to feel lighter, think more clearly, and tend to enjoy every little thing in life so much more. I see an increase in my vitality; my hair and skin look healthier, and my eyes shine brighter.

This valuable lesson is something that I've learned over the years by abstaining from consuming sugary foods for periods of time such as the 40 days of lent or for 2 months before the festive season. The first 3 weeks can be challenging as my body has cravings for them, but powering through is always worth it because I feel so good after! Not only does my body feel clean, healthy, and vibrant, but my mental health gets a boost too. It's very empowering, satisfying, and rewarding to take some time for yourself to reset.

Processed foods contain refined carbohydrates, sugars, too much salt, and artificial sweeteners such as aspartame. These ingredients have little or no nutritional value and are known to have negative effects on our moods, as well as our bodies. They can trigger feelings of anxiety, irritability, and brain fog, as well as worsening depression and contributing to insomnia.

I used to have a can of diet fizzy drink every day with my lunch, and I used to regularly suffer from unexplained panic attacks. When I gave up fizzy drinks for lent one year my panic attacks ceased and my anxiety levels reduced - a surprising result which piqued my curiosity regarding the effect that the things we consume have on our mental health. For this reason I now listen to my body, and I choose to take better care of myself. This is why I count 'nutrition' as one of my positivity practices, and I know that it can help all us to improve our health and wellbeing.

Our nervous and immune systems are linked to our gut-brain connection. The brain and the gut are in constant communication with each other; we often observe how nervousness, anxiety or stress can cause an upset tummy, or sudden changes of appetite. When we are mentally or emotionally upset, it can have a direct impact on our physical health. Recent scientific research is now revealing that this also happens with poor nutrition - what we eat and drink has a direct impact on our mood. The gut sends signals to the brain which then triggers the release of hormones within the body. Surprisingly, most of the body's 'feel-good' hormone serotonin is produced in the gut, rather than the brain! This knowledge is valuable because it reenforces the fact that our diets are an important contributing factor when it comes to supporting our mental and emotional health.

Diving deeper into this subject, I feel it's valuable to share the positive impact that getting tested for food intolerances can have on our lives; as a child I was asthmatic and in my late teens I suffered severe hayfever. It's often been reported that both of these health issues could be connected to, or at least potentially aggravated by food intolerances. It's interesting to observe that after I got tested by a homeopath and followed their recommendations, my symptoms of both conditions massively reduced.

Intolerances are less serious than allergies, but they can cause uncomfortable and inconvenient symptoms within the body that make us feel unwell. We are all different and our own individual experiences with nutrition will be just as unique, and as ever-changing as we are ourselves. Personally speaking, these issues come in the form of experiencing eczema, stomach aches, bloating and digestive issues. Permanently cutting out our trigger foods is unwise as it can be counterproductive but reducing our intake of them in accordance with professional advice is very beneficial for our health. Aside from our personal experiences, one of the major benefits of becoming aware of our intolerances and adjusting our diets accordingly, is that our digestive system will become more robust. A healthier digestive system is supportive to improving immune function, which generally leads to a healthier body, and that in turn helps to cultivate a healthier, happier mindset.

Diets are a personal thing. What's right for me, isn't necessarily right for you, nor for anyone else. I would encourage everyone to explore what is good for themselves, and what is appropriate and healthy for their own body, and to make healthy lifestyle and especially nutritional choices accordingly. I would also recommend seeking professional advice and guidance before making any major changes.

I believe that taking good care of ourselves is an act of self-love. Let us strive for a healthy balance between providing the body with the daily nutrients it needs to thrive, and enjoying the occasional indulgences which give us pleasure.

Positivity in practice

What unhealthy choice can you leave out today?

Pick at least one and choose to leave it out just for today. Give yourself credit at the end of the day if you successfully achieve this goal. Don't beat yourself too much if you don't, you can always try again tomorrow.
If you succeed, and decide to leave it out again tomorrow, well done!

What healthy choice can you add?

Maybe it's to eat more fruit, veg or nuts, or it could be to hydrate well, or reduce your portion size. Golden paste is very good for us. If don't already know about it, perhaps you would like to research it for yourself and give it a try. Choose at least one extra healthy option today, and don't forget to applaud yourself afterwards

Check your supplements

Have you taken your vitamins today? Maybe you need to review or renew them. If you don't already take any, perhaps this is a good time to start…

Dare to try something new

Next time you go food shopping, or are dining out, choose something different from the shelves or menu. Make it a healthy option, and preferably something you've never tried before!

Self-Love

The most important relationship you'll ever have, is the one you have with yourself

It has never been more talked about nor so widely accepted as being essential for our wellbeing, so it's no wonder then, that self-love is a foundational positivity practice. Our physical energy levels and positivity mindset can be boosted massively by cultivating a good self-love relationship and a healthy self-care routine. When we fill our own cup first, we are then able to give more to others - both within our personal relationships and also among our community.

Self-love practices are healthy habits for the body, mind, heart, and soul, and they should become a way of life, not just a one off or occasional thing.

Let's break it down and begin with the body; I see self-care as the act of taking good care of ourselves and especially tending to our most basic and daily physical needs. It sounds so simple and yet we often forget to focus on things like whether we have drunk enough water today. Ask yourself that question right now, and if you have a drink nearby, take a sip. There's no time like the present to love ourselves. What about the body's other needs - are we supporting it by eating the right nutrients, taking regular exercise, and getting a sufficient amount of rest? Resting is just as important as exercising because getting the right amount of quality rest supports brain function.

The simple act of keeping our bodies and our homes clean is important for hygiene reasons, and at the same time can feel really nurturing to do. Washing ourselves daily, cleaning our teeth properly, opening the windows and vacuuming the house are the kind of things that we often take for granted or think of as a chore, and yet they are so good for us. It's empowering to take care of and love ourselves.

Aside from our fundamental basic needs, we all sometimes need a little something extra. Whether it's to help support our physical health or to treat ourselves to a bit of pampering, it's important to carve out some dedicated time for ourselves each week.

Friday night is my self-care and solitude night. I might have an extra luxurious bath, listen to jazz music and read a book, or simply paint my nails. It varies from week to week depending on what I need or feel like doing. Whatever I choose to do, I silence my phone and make sure I make the most of this quality time just for me! It always involves an early night and I've come to love taking care of myself this way.

What about the extras then? We all need an occasional break and a change of scenery from time to time (and we all deserve a treat). Whether that means taking an adventure holiday, enjoying a relaxing retreat, or indulging in a quick spa treatment, it is an act of self-love to pencil in time for rewards and to enjoy looking forward to them.

I'm a huge fan of complementary and holistic therapies, not only as occasional treats but as essentials which can help improve our health and overall quality of life. There are times when we might need to seek the services of independent professionals to help us treat and recover from injuries or illness. While they might cost us financially, they are a worthwhile investment in our long-term health and healing. These include things such as physiotherapy, chiropractic treatments, acupuncture, and reflexology, etc. There are many, many different types of complementary treatments available and it's worth taking some time to research them and get a consultation from a suitably qualified practitioner. Nourishing our basic needs is a long-term and sustainable way of life. A healthy body is supportive to a healthy mindset and forms an excellent foundation from which we can build deeper self-love practices. These fundamental requirements extend beyond tending to our physical needs, they include mental and emotional self-care too.

A quick and effective self-love exercise which can benefit our mental and emotional wellbeing is to write down all the sources of love in our lives. So often when we are stressed, anxious, or grieving the loss of a relationship (be that through heartbreak or the passing of a loved one), we habitually focus on what we've lost, rather than reminding ourselves of what we still have. Taking a few minutes to make a list of all the people in your life who you love, or who love you, can help to shift your perspective. Additionally, if you also list the places you love to go and all of the things you love to do, it is possible to uplift your mood and further cultivate a gratitude mindset.

Becoming aware of the way in which we speak to, and about, ourselves is essential to a positivity mindset and lifestyle. I invite you to pay attention to your internal dialogue - how are you speaking about yourself, both within your own mind and when speaking to other people? We all have times when we criticise or doubt ourselves, and that is perfectly natural, but it's important not to feed those thoughts for too long or allow them to become habitual thinking patterns. We can counteract them with techniques that include positive affirmations, meditation, and mindfulness. In some cases, more professional help such as cognitive behavioural therapy may be useful, but in general these self-administered well-being tools can be very effective on their own.

Positive affirmations, meditation, and mindfulness practices can be used in building confidence and self-esteem, improving the relationship we have with ourselves as well as with others. If we don't value ourselves, we will struggle to allow other people to value us too. When we respect and believe in ourselves, we demonstrate that's how we want and expect others to behave towards us. We also set a good example for the people in our lives who look up to us as mentors and inspirational role models.

As well as improving our mental health, self-love practices are beneficial for our emotional wellbeing. When we are faced with life's challenging circumstances and stressful situations, it's easy to become energetically and emotionally drained without even realising it. Whilst we can't change the fact that we'll face many challenges throughout life, we can rely on our wellbeing tools to help build resilience, increase self-awareness, and prevent us becoming emotionally "overdrawn".

Spending time in solitude for reflection and contemplation, and the restoration of energy levels is self-love in practice. Sometimes we need a little bit of time to face, feel, and process our thoughts and emotions instead of resisting or avoiding them. Journaling and meditation are both good tools for this. Nurturing our emotional health is very healing. It helps us to develop self-acceptance and to progress our personal and spiritual growth along the way.

Spending time nourishing our spirituality and soaking up 'soul food' is also incredibly good for us. This can mean different things to different people, so it's important to use discernment and follow your own path and to do so at your own pace. It's not a race or competition, it's a life-long journey and can be very rewarding. We can gain a real sense of purpose through spiritual pursuits, and we can connect to the deeper source of divine love that exists far beyond ourselves.

Self-love is a vast and varied subject, and it can be subcategorised into many other practices in their own right. All of my positivity practices can be classed as self-love in one way or another and using them regularly can help us to flow through life in a more peaceful, contented, and well-balanced way. We'll dive deeper into some more of them in the following chapters.

Positivity in practice

Prioritise your self care

Dedicate a regular time to have some quality time for yourself and use it to do something that nourishes your own needs. This could be something simple or indulgent as little as 30 minutes or an entire day. Make it a regular weekly or monthly occurrence.

Reflect on the sources of love in your life

Make a list of all the people, places and things in your life that you love. Take a few minutes to reflect, appreciate and feel the love in your life.

Love

- **Where?** (where do I love to be?)
- **What?** (what do you love doing?)
- **Pets**
- **Family**
- **Who?**
- **Friends**
- **Others** (Colleagues, teachers, role models, etc.)

Write yourself a love letter

Spend 10 minutes writing yourself a love letter, or a list of all the things you love about yourself. Afterwards take a look in the mirror and read it out loud to yourself. Then look into your own eyes and smile.

Fill a jar full of love

If you find it particularly challenging to love yourself, you could ask your closest family & friends to write something they love about you, on small pieces of paper. Add them all to a jar and decorate it - perhaps with a heart. Anytime you need a little pick me up, open the jar and read the love notes.

Treat yourself to a gift

Buy or pick yourself some flowers, a candle, or your favourite chocolates… anything that you consider to be a treat for yourself, no matter how small.

Use the colour pink to improve your relationship with yourself

Wear something pink, carry a piece of rose quartz or use something pink within your daily tasks.

Create a self-love affirmation

Write or choose a positive phrase that resonates with you and say it every day either out loud or in your mind. If you can't think of one yourself, here are some suggestions…

'I love and accept myself, exactly as I am'
'I believe in myself'
'I am beautiful'
'I am loved'

Setting Boundaries

Know your values, set your limits, and learn to get comfortable saying 'no'

Setting boundaries can be considered an act of self-love. Sometimes we need some time out for ourselves; whether it's to restore our energy, dedicate time to achieving a goal, or simply to help establish a healthy work/life balance. We may occasionally need to turn down an invitation that we don't want to accept or say 'no' to something because it goes against our values. These are all examples of setting boundaries, which I believe is an essential practice that can help us to protect and maintain our vitality, health, and happiness.

It's a positivity practice which can be challenging to begin with, especially for those of us who tend to be 'people-pleasers' or as yet lack the confidence to speak up for ourselves. Like anything else though, it becomes easier and more natural, with practice. It nourishes and strengthens our relationship with ourselves, as well as others, boosts confidence levels and leaves us feeling empowered.

Discovering which boundaries we need to establish in our lives, requires us to regularly check in and reflect within ourselves and upon our surroundings. It's important to become aware of who or what is depleting our own energy. With this awareness we can then choose what positive action can be put in place to prevent or lessen this effect. Think of the act of setting boundaries as a well-being energy defence system.

Has anyone ever told you that it's okay to limit the amount of time you spend around people or situations which drain you? If not, let me be the first to tell you that it is perfectly okay to say "no" to people, without having to apologise or explain yourself. You don't have to please other people at the expense of your own happiness. It's okay to express your needs and values, and to uphold them.

Maybe you think it's easier said than done, right? So, let's perhaps start with a few small things which can make a big difference…

Sometimes we just need some time to think and a bit of breathing space, preferably alone and without being disturbed or distracted. Silencing or switching off our phones is a great place to start. We don't need to be available 24/7. Replying to messages or returning missed calls later is perfectly acceptable. Relaxing activities such as taking a bath or walking our dogs without being on our phone at the same time, makes the experience much more pleasurable and calming.

Multitasking seems to have become expected of us, and whilst it often appears that we can achieve more or save time, by doing so, it can actually have the opposite effect. It can raise our stress levels, cause confusion, and lead to distractions. Instead, consciously choosing to put our 'to do' lists aside for a little while enables us to think more clearly and preserves our energy, which actually helps us to become more productive! For example, chatting to someone on the phone whilst trying to organise some paperwork will slow down the process as well as increase the likelihood of a mistake being made, requiring us to go back later and spend even more time correcting it. Both the mistake and the need to fix it will increase our stress levels, which could have been avoided had we maintained that boundary of focusing on the task at hand without answering the phone.

When spending time online, we can choose which social media accounts to follow or more importantly - unfollow. Taking stock of the kind of content we are regularly being influenced by, and noticing how it makes us feel, will help us to decide what we need to see less of.

Having a digital de-clutter is really good for our mental health, so feel free to hide, unfollow or delete any accounts which are having a negative impact on you.

We can do the same when it comes to choosing what we watch on TV or the kind of music we listen to; it's okay to switch off the news if it makes us feel anxious, or we can simply decide to watch it less often. We can pay attention to what kind of music uplifts or soothes us, rather than enduring something which makes us feel tense or agitated. We can consciously choose to listen to more of the feel-good stuff. I personally like relaxing to jazz music in the evenings when I'm at home - it helps me to unwind. I often choose to play music instead of watching TV, because it makes me feel good.
For our mental and emotional well-being, and for the benefit of our

relationships with others, I believe it's really important to set boundaries with and around people. Although spending time with some people uplifts and energises us, being around others can mentally and physically drain us. For example, if someone is constantly moaning, complaining, or saying negative things, they're likely to be unpleasant to be around. They will test our patience and tire us out more quickly than if we spend time with someone who's optimistic, cheerful, and whose company we find enjoyable. Whilst it's not always possible to completely avoid the people who have a negative impact on us, it is sometimes possible to restrict the amount of time we spend with them.

There are times when we must speak up for ourselves when it comes to upholding boundaries in order to protect our wellbeing, and that's ok. It's ok to let our colleagues know that we're on our break time and would prefer not to be disturbed, or to not accept an invitation to see a friend if we've already got several other things planned that week.

Overloading our diaries or overworking our bodies leaves us feeling worn out, grumpy, and fed up. It's ok to say 'no' to people, or to express the fact that you're having a self-care night - not having plans with other people doesn't mean that we have to be available if an invitation comes, especially if we need to have some downtime for ourselves.

Setting healthy boundaries for our ourselves is a great preventative against burn out and enables us to strengthen our relationships with others. Our loved ones will get used to us setting boundaries for ourselves and learn to respect our choices. They might even follow our lead and begin to establish some boundaries for themselves too.

Although I'm a people-person and enjoy spending time with others, I'm very much an introvert by nature. I love to spend quality time alone when I can process my thoughts, and I love quiet-time because it helps me to decompress and reenergise. It allows me to show up as the best version of myself when reconnecting with others, be it when socialising or working. I have learned how beneficial it is to literally pencil in time for solitude in my calendar, and the importance of sticking to it. I always take a proper lunch break when I'm at work, regardless of how busy I am because I know the quality of my work would suffer if I didn't.

Many of us can find it exhausting to spend too long around people in general, especially if we are empathic or highly sensitive. It can be too stimulating to be among large groups of people or to be in busy, loud places. Becoming aware of this is really valuable, as it helps us to understand our needs, and establishing boundaries around this can help us to organise our self care time. Finding the right balance between being around others, and having enough downtime will improve our physical, mental, and emotional wellbeing.

As well as finding time for ourselves, it's also really important to carve out time to rest properly. I'm not talking about sleep- but actual rest. It's essential in order for our bodies to recharge, repair and restore. This can help to prevent burnout and provide our body with the opportunity to heal. Think of it as like needing to recharge the battery on your phone - if you don't plug it in and let it do its thing, it won't perform optimally. Our bodies need time to rest and recharge, and it's important that we realise that, unlike our phones, we can't just buy a new battery or replace the handset when it's reached the end of its lifespan. We've each got just one, irreplaceable body to carry us through this life, so we need to make taking good care of it a priority.

I have mentioned before that one of my favourite positivity practices is my "self-care night"- for me that looks like having a regular Friday night to myself. It's a lovely time of solitude, relaxation and restoration that has become a ritual that I really look forward to. It's a healthy habit and personal boundary that I rarely compromise on and often involves some kind of pampering or treat, a long hot bath and always an early night. It might involve playing relaxing music, practicing yin yoga, or cooking something delicious, with my phone switched to silent so that I can enjoy a quality relaxing night. Doing this restores my energy levels, makes me feel cheerful the next morning, and enables me to show up as the best version of myself for others. Taking time to take care of myself makes me a better friend, partner, and family member.

A healthy boundary which is highly recommended by both scientists and medical professionals is to switch off all electronic devices by 10pm, and ideally not having them in the bedroom at all. For example, I choose not to have a TV upstairs in my home. The use of electronic devices at bedtime has a negative and damaging impact on our health; melatonin is the sleep hormone that regulates our circadian rhythm (the natural cycle of day and night which governs our waking and sleep cycles). It is naturally produced by the body as we prepare for sleep but becomes suppressed when using electronic devices. The stimulation of looking at screens late at night is disruptive to our sleep patterns and leaves us feeling drained the next day, triggering an increase of cortisol aka 'the stress hormone'. It can also cause problems with eye health, hormonal imbalances, reduced cognitive brain function and cause irritable moods.

To help combat this, it is advised that we switch off electronic devices 30 mins before sleep and to keep them at least 3 feet (1 metre) away from our bodies. Doing so is said to reduce our exposure to electromagnetic field (EMF) pollution, which is a mild form of energy radiation given off by electronic devices. EMF is known to have a negative impact on our health at a cellular level, and too much exposure can cause long term issues such as migraines, skin problems, fatigue, and weakened immune systems.

Establishing a regular and healthy bedtime routine is one of the best things we can do for ourselves as it will help the body to slow down, calm the nervous system, and automatically produce melatonin. This will assist us to settle into a good night's sleep and enable us to wake better in the morning, setting us up nicely for the day ahead.

Setting healthy boundaries around our eating habits is highly beneficial, as I have already mentioned in the chapter on nutrition, but paying attention to when we eat is just as valuable. It is advised that we stop eating 3 hours before we go to sleep because if the body is digesting food late at night, the brain is more active, and it'll have a detrimental effect on our ability to fall and stay asleep.

As you can see, there are many ways in which setting boundaries can help us to make small changes that come with big improvements to our well-being, and the above-mentioned ones are just a few examples. As individuals, we all have different needs, and our personal boundaries will vary greatly. They will also naturally change over time along with our circumstances. I recommend experimenting with yours by applying a "trial and error" approach. Take your time, observe what works well for you, and remember that it's perfectly ok to change your mind about anything that isn't working in your favour.

One of the best suggestions I can offer to help us maintain this positivity practice is being organised with your time management. Being organised with our time, and preparing anything we need to do in advance to support that is really valuable. It can help us to find calm instead of chaos, to feel motivated instead of exhausted, and to allow us to flow through life more easily.

Positivity in practice

Say 'No'

Politely say no to someone or something, without apologising or feeling the need to explain yourself.

Notifications: OFF

Switch your phone on silent and simply be unavailable for a duration of time, such as when you're having a meal or reading a book.

Have an early night

Go offline, switch off the TV and enjoy a quality early night for yourself.

Have a digital detox

Unfollow some social media accounts that are no longer having a positive impact on you.

Positive Influences

Be mindful of who/what you surround yourself with

Whether we are aware of it or not, the people we find ourselves with, and the places and circumstances we find ourselves in, all have some kind of subconscious influence on our minds and emotions. Our personal and work relationships, choice of the social media accounts we follow, what we're watching on TV, and the music we listen to, all affect us in some way. Sometimes it's really obvious, while other times it can be more subtle, but everything around us has an effect on our physiology, state of mind, and overall well-being. Mindfully and deliberately paying attention to how these things make us feel enables us to become aware of the impact they are having on our lives and can help us to determine whether we are being negatively affected or positively influenced.

For example, think of someone who you know who is angry a lot of the time, perhaps they are always saying negative things about others. Imagine you see them in them in the street coming towards you - what are your first thoughts and how does it make you feel? Perhaps your body tenses up and your natural reaction is to want to avoid them?! Oh yes - we've all been there. That's an obvious and negative reaction, and your body and mind already want you to spend as little time as possible interacting with that person.

Now bring to mind the image of someone who you enjoy talking to, a person who makes you laugh or smile. Do you notice a difference in your body? Maybe you're actually smiling right now at the thought of them. Clearly, they have a positive impact you, and after an enjoyable chat with them, you'll most likely walk away feeling uplifted and happy. This is likely to influence your mood for the better, as you go about the rest of your day and you naturally find yourself wanting to spend time with them in future.

Whilst setting boundaries for ourselves is a great practice which reduces the impact of being exposed to negative influences, spending time focusing on the positive influences around us can only serve to improve our mood, health and quality of life. Therefore, spending more time in the company of people who make us feel good, has a positive impact on our wellbeing. The same can be said for our media choices; watching uplifting television shows and movies such as comedies or inspirational stories gives us that feel-good factor, while watching drama, horror, or violence can cause our bodies to react with the stress response.

Listening to the music which makes us feel good, rather than agitated and tense, will have a calming effect on our nervous systems - surely it makes sense to choose these positive influences more often.

Of course, eliminating all negativity from our lives is both unrealistic and impossible, and I'm not suggesting that you even attempt to achieve this. What I am suggesting is that we strive for a level where we actively encourage more positive, than negative influences around us. Doing so will help keep us motivated and inspired, and feel more balanced- remember the key word here is 'practice'. Positive influences make us feel energised and lighter, both physically and mentally. Negative influences make us feel tense and heavy in the body, lowering our mood and emotional state.

It's not all about people, tv, and social media accounts, although that's a good place to start. Our actual physical surroundings can positively influence our well-being too; from our homes and places of work to social environments and even the area in which we live. Something as simple as opening the curtains to let the light in, being in a clean and nicely decorated building, or enjoying a lovely outdoor view in our neighbourhood can all contribute to our levels of happiness.

Energy flows where focus goes, so let's take a moment to focus on our home; Unclean and cluttered homes have a negative impact on our mental health and emotional state, so it's wise to ensure that our homes are a place in which we enjoy returning to. Keeping it clean and filling it with positive influences will uplift us and give us a sense of satisfaction. It's also an act of self care. We might want to consider displaying photos of our favourite people, places, role models, or pets. Hanging something like an inspirational quote or a vision board on the wall where we can see it every day will subtly influence us in a positive way. It can help us to stay motivated and inspired.

Choosing light or bright colours within our decor is good for us, being in dark and dimly lit surroundings is draining. If you have a garden and enjoy being out there in it, make it a more inviting and enjoyable place to spend time in - clear the weeds, cut the grass, and add some beautiful plants. Our subconscious minds respond to all of these influencing factors, which in turn has an uplifting effect on our health and happiness.

We can't all control our work environments, but perhaps there's a few things we can do to improve the positive energy that flows there, such as displaying a visual reminder of goals that we have achieved (or wish to achieve). This can help us to find motivation on the tough days. We might like to place a positive quote or inspirational picture in a place where we can see it regularly, these kinds of images can help to boost our energy levels and have an uplifting effect on our moods. Regularly decluttering and keeping our work area tidy, will help us to feel calm and enable us to think more clearly. We could also try focusing on appreciating those colleagues who uplift us and express our gratitude towards them - this is a great way to build and strengthen teamwork, increasing positive energy within the workplace.

Whichever way we choose to surround ourselves with positive influences, we will improve our wellbeing, but never underestimate the power that YOU have to be a positive influence. You can uplift others with a simple smile, hold the door open for someone or be sure to say 'thank you' at every opportunity. Positive energy is infectious, so let's become aware of the influences in our life and choose to surround ourselves as much as possible with the positive ones.

Positivity in practice

Hang a picture or poster of someone or something that positively influences you

It could be a family member, friend, celebrity role model, or something like an affirmation or inspiring quote. Using a screensaver or wallpaper on your electronic device is also an option.

Write down your intentions and goals

Make a list of your intentions and goals and place it somewhere that you can see them every day. Tick off each item as you successfully achieve your goals.

Create a vision board

Fill it with images that inspire, motivate, and positively influence you. Make it bright, colourful and cheerful. Display it somewhere you'll see it every single day.

Choose something new to follow on social media

Find an account whose feed is predominantly filled with content that you consider to be a positive influence, and subscribe to or follow their account. Maybe you could set a notifications to pop-up each time they make a new post.

Generosity

Get into the spirit of giving with a generous heart

A grateful heart leads to a generous heart. With this positivity practice, I invite you to see what happens when we give our time and energy to others; be it family, friends, strangers, our community, or the environment.

Whether we are aware of it or not, our moods and behaviours have a knock-on effect on other people. All mental and emotional states emit an energetic frequency that the typical human eye cannot see, but the energy of it can be felt by others. Have you ever seen someone laughing and have found yourself smiling or laughing along with them, even if you don't know why? Or perhaps you can recall a time when you've been around someone who's grumpy or angry and found that their foul mood has made you feel grumpy too? These are easily identifiable examples of how our own mood can have an impact on other people.

This is why it's wise for us to be mindful of how we are, especially around others, and to make a choice about the kind of energy we're putting out there. In the same way that a yawn or a smile can be contagious, so can our positive emotions, thoughts, words and actions, such as happiness, kindness, and generosity of spirit. Every single one of us has the potential to make a positive difference in someone else's day, so can you imagine the possibilities we could create by cultivating a generous heart?

This doesn't necessarily mean donating money or material goods to charitable causes (which is of course, a generous and kind thing to do), it can mean simply giving your time and attention to someone else. There are many ways in which we can uplift other people; perhaps it might be to inspire and motivate them, make them feel valued and listened to, or leave them feeling joyful after a humorous interaction.

These gestures of generosity might include something as small or seemingly insignificant as holding a door open for a stranger, saying hello to a neighbour, or paying someone a compliment. Generosity can be asking someone how they are and genuinely listening to their response. Simply looking into another person's eyes as they speak can provide them with a sense of connection and make them feel valued. There are times when we all need someone to talk to, we might not be necessarily looking for an answer or solution to our worries, but rather a friendly ear to just listen. Wouldn't it be nice to be that person whom someone else can offload to, and to be able to give them that sense of support?

Helping others just because you can, without any expectation in return, is a wonderful way to give your time and energy generously, as well as an opportunity to positively contribute to the spirit within your community. Kindness, compassion, and love are all qualities that the world needs more of. Having emphasised that, allow me to share with you some of the ways in which giving can be good for us too; studies have shown that generosity actually promotes better health! It reduces the risk of dementia, lowers depression and helps to manage chronic pain - it can even increase our life span! Another byproduct of acting with generosity it that it can build a sense of connection to our communities and improves our relationships with others.

Think of a time when you needed some help but there was no one to turn to and you didn't know what to do- perhaps you felt despair, fear or loneliness. In times like these we often long for someone to come along to help us.

Now think of a time when someone did help you and try to clearly remember how you felt as a result of their actions and attitude towards you - perhaps you felt a sense of relief and gratitude or, at the very least, less alone and more reassured.

Wouldn't it be nice to give another person that same sense of relief, support or connection, just because you can?

Over the years I've learned many tools and techniques which can reduce anxiety. Nowadays, I love to share them with others because I know it will help them and will bring relief to their symptoms. I only wish someone had shown me these things 20 years ago when I was suffering from panic attacks and needed them the most!

There are times when we all feel utterly helpless. We will naturally go through challenging circumstances in life, many of which are out of our control. It's during these times that it can be transformational to focus on helping others instead of continuously stewing over our own troubles.

Being of service to others can help us to feel like we are being proactive in producing a positive outcome for another cause. My mum is great example of this; she's very empathic and can get herself really upset by the misfortunes of others. One day she realised that her frustration at not being able to fix other people's problems was having a detrimental effect on her own health and well-being and so, she decided to do something about it by taking up litter-picking! It has a positive impact on her own health because it gets her some fresh air and outdoor exercise, as well as doing something good for the local environment. It enables her to channel her stress energy into something more productive, whilst giving her a sense of purpose and satisfaction.

Another great benefit is, that it nourishes her spirituality. She says it makes her feel connected to nature and closer to God. She often sends out prayers while she's litter-picking and always goes home feeling more uplifted than when she set out. She gets a lot of thanks from strangers for what she does too and although this isn't why she does it, it is rewarding for her nonetheless. She feels a sense of satisfaction from having made a positive contribution to the local community and environment.

Activities like this can help us to gain mental clarity and improve our ability to make decisions, as well as boosting our confidence and self-esteem. Helping others contributes to our own self-care too. It can help us to shift our perspective, increasing our compassion for others and making us less selfish.

After separating from my ex-partner several years ago, I decided to find a local walking group to join. My timing was perfect because there was a new one starting up just as I was buying my new home and looking for ways to build a new life for myself. As a socially anxious person I had been nervous about meeting everyone for the first time and almost talked myself out of going before I even got to the first walk... but you know what I'm going to say next don't you?

That's right - I needn't have worried because most of the others felt the same way too! I'm really glad I made myself go that day because it changed my life for the better in so many ways; I joined with the intention of discovering new walking routes within the safety of a group and hoped at best, to connect with some like-minded people. I ended up meeting some great friends who became like family! We enjoyed sharing weekend adventures and discovering new places together. Many of us gained new confidence too as we began to socialise together. We found a sense of connection and support as we journeyed through the ups and downs of the next chapter of our lives together. I also used to have a fear of speaking in public, which some friends helped me to overcome by encouraging me to teach them yoga whilst on holiday. I credit their belief in me to giving me the confidence to train as an official instructor. The more I practiced with friends, the more I began to believe in myself and my capabilities - I also found myself having a lot of fun too! I learned to trust my own voice and to laugh at myself when I get tongue-tied. It's not the end of the world if we stumble over our words, and in fact, it makes us more relatable to others because it happens to us all!

Community spirit

Most humans long to belong and being part of a community or a social group can be very beneficial to our well-being, especially for those of us who have lost loved ones or don't have family nearby. Community spirit can provide us with a sense of belonging and purpose, helping us to feel supported, safe, welcome, and nourished. It can help to reduce feelings of stress, loneliness, anxiety, and depression. We can feel less isolated and more closely connected to part of something much bigger than ourselves when we open our hearts to the community around us.

I invite you to ask yourself, what can I contribute to my local community? How can I get involved? While there are many social groups out there, there are also local opportunities where you can help or volunteer within your neighbourhood and surrounding area. We can find a variety of information in places such as community centres, libraries, and churches. It can also be helpful to get in touch with organisations such as local councils, countryside rangers, and leisure centres. Many of which can be found via social media platforms.

Cultivating a generous heart and helping others is one of the most uplifting and rewarding things we can do for ourselves, as well as for other people. We can improve our own well-being, make personal growth breakthroughs, and lead by example for others. Like a domino effect, generosity of spirit, no matter how small, has the potential to have far-reaching, positive consequences. Every single one of us can contribute to making the world a better place by inspiring generosity, so let's get to it…

Positivity in practice

Offer assistance to a loved one

Check on a friend, family member or neighbour and see if there's something you can help them with.

Give someone a homemade gift

Make or draw something by hand and give it to someone you care about.

Perform an act of kindness for a stranger

It could be paying for someone else's coffee as you buy your own, holding the door open for someone or simply asking how someone is at the bus stop.

Do something positive for the benefit of your local community

This could be volunteering at a local organisation or something as small as litter picking, adding something to the food bank or cleaning up an extra poop when you're out walking your own dog.

Take action to inspire children or young people

Choose any activity from the list above, or something of your own choosing and do it with, or in the presence of the younger generation. Be a positive influence for them and encourage them to be a postive influence for others, too.

Colour

Enhance your daily life with the use of colour

Colours are bright, cheerful, and expressive. We use them all the time to decorate our homes, style our wardrobes and enjoy creative projects- it can be so much fun! But did you know that colour can be used in a therapeutic way to enhance our well-being?

"Colour Therapy" sounds very modern, but it dates all the way back as far as the ancient Egyptians! For thousands of years, across different continents, people have used colour as a tool for healing purposes.

In recent times we have mostly used colour as a form of self-expression, such as in fashion or interior design, but with complimentary therapies becoming increasingly popular, colour therapy is once again being used in a professional way for holistic purposes.

Colour subtly impacts the subconscious mind, which has a psychological effect on our mental and emotional health. It also has the ability to assist the physical body in healing by triggering the brain to respond accordingly, depending on the body's needs. It can be used in calming ways to soothe the nervous system and induce relaxation, or stimulating ways to uplift our mood and boost energy levels. Whatever we need, there's a colour that can help!

Generally speaking, warm colours such as red, orange, and yellow are uplifting and energising. Cool colours such as purple, blue, and green are soothing and calming. It's important to be mindful of how we use colour though, because too much over too long of a period can be counterproductive; for example, red is a strong colour which is good for helping us to feel grounded, safe, and secure but if used too strongly it can result in us becoming irritated or angry. Blue has a cooling effect which is brilliant for calming a bad temper or soothing a headache, but if we spend too much time with it, we might notice a negative drop in our mood and energy levels - an effect that is commonly referred to "having the blues". Finding a healthy, balanced way of using colour is the most beneficial and effective way to harness its therapeutic qualities.

The use of colour can be applied in a variety of ways, many techniques of which can be combined to create 'layers' of holistic support. Whilst there are more specialised colour-healing techniques such as chromotherapy, chakra healing, and aura reading which should be carried out by a qualified professional, there many practical ways in which we can use colour therapy for ourselves and incorporate it into our everyday lives, in order to improve our health and well-being.

One of the easiest ways to influence our mood with colour is through our daily choice of clothing, accessories, and décor. The colours we wear and are surrounded by, will subtly affect how we think, feel, and interact with others. I invite you to begin to become aware of the colours in your homes, places of work, public spaces, and even your garden. Perhaps spend a little time observing the colours around you and notice how they make you feel.

For example, yellow is cheerful and can be used to boost energy and confidence. I've noticed that whenever I wear yellow, people always smile at me more and they often comment on how nice I look. It's a happy colour which uplifts my mood and seems to have an uplifting effect on other people too. I'm certain that the response wouldn't happen if I were to wear grey, so I choose not to do- I simply don't like it, find it to be dull, and it's known to trigger feelings of depression. I recommend wearing yellow if you're feeling shy or a little sluggish, and if wearing it as a block colour feels a touch too bold, then perhaps try gently incorporating it into some accessories instead.

The ancient Egyptians used to paint chambers in solid colours, for varying purposes and would lay down to relax in them for a period of time. When we fully immerse ourselves in one colour, it's called 'colour-bathing'. It's a technique that is generally used when healing is required, or when we need to bring about a particular quality or energy that we've been lacking. I once painted my bedroom pink to help myself heal from a broken heart. I found it really comforting to "bathe" in this nourishing colour as I discovered my ability to love myself and restore my emotional health.

These days my bedroom is painted a soft shade of green. I chose it because it's the best colour to promote balance and harmony. It's both soothing and restful, and yet uplifting and inspiring. It pairs well with the colour white, which is the colour of my furniture. White contains all the colours of the spectrum and even though our eyes can't see them, the subconscious mind can still perceive them. Therefore, white can be used alongside any colour to support it.

'Complementary Colours' are colours which work really well together. These are pairs of colours which sit opposite each other on the colour wheel (the spectrum of colour that was originally mapped into a circle and was created in the 17th century by Sir Isaac Newton!) They are red and green, orange and blue, yellow and purple. They complement each other by working with the theory that opposites attract. Not only do they visually look good together, but they also have a positive psychological effect when used in pairs. For example, an artistic person who owns some kind of creative business will need stay inspired whilst remaining clear-headed. They could infuse some colour into their surroundings by using orange to get their creative juices flowing and use blue to help them calmly make decisions and communicate well with others. When used together, complementary colours will strengthen the attributes of one another.

It's not just the colour of the walls that influence our moods, we can use colour therapy through interior design in more gentle ways too; a plain room can be livened up with splash of colour by using textiles such as cushions, curtains, lampshades and bedding etc. or with even smaller items like candles, vases or picture frames.

Decor and clothing are good places to start, but there's so much more to colour therapy; other applications include using it in meditation and mindfulness practices; mindful colouring has become popular in recent times, and it can also be used in art therapy sessions. In meditation, we often use colour in visualisation and guided relaxation techniques to support the purpose of the session.

Using aromatherapy is a fantastic method too; lavender is purple, which is a deeply soothing colour, so we can use the scent of lavender to help us relax. Essential oils, candles, or room sprays are a quick and easy way to apply an additional holistic 'layer' of colour therapy.

We can even use colour in when choosing our food; bananas boost our energy levels as does the colour yellow. Oranges are full of vitamin c, which helps to boost our vitality - the colour orange is associated with vibrancy. Blueberries are known to reduce inflammation - blue is a calming and soothing colour. Colour is one of my favourite positivity practices and an enjoyable tool that is both easily accessible and extremely versatile. I invite you to bring more colour into your life and notice the fantastic ways it can support your health, well-being and mindset. Turn the page for a quick and easy colour guide to get you started.

Red

Physical

Stimulates physical energy, circulation, menstruation & ovulation.

Increases blood pressure. Promotes good heart health & blood quality.

Combats fatigue.

Mental & Emotional

Promotes assertiveness, passion, ambition, and sexual attraction.

Grounding

Supports feelings of stability & security.

Spiritual

Promotes strength.

Supports love.

Orange

Physical

Increases physical vitality.

Activates lungs & thyroid gland.

Strengthens stomach & cell renewal.

Mental & Emotional

Promotes creativity, joy, and feelings of freedom.

Increases enthusiasm and optimism.

Decreases negativity.

Spiritual

Increases compassion and protection.

Aids success and prosperity.

Yellow

Physical

Strengthens the nervous system.

Stimulates the lymphatic & digestion systems.

Cleanses the liver & intestines.

Mental & emotional

Fun, energising and motivating.

Increases confidence and self-worth.

Promotes hope & optimism

Spiritual

Connects to personal power & inner strength.

Enhances enlightenment and personal growth.

Green

Physical

Aids the heart and circulatory system.

Supports the lungs & respiratory system.

Increases fertility.

Mental & emotional

Soothing

Supports recovery and healing.

Brings about balance and harmony

Spiritual

Connects to nature. Enhances rebirth & new beginnings.

Aids transformation. Increases luck & attracts abundance.

Pink

Physical

Aids healing

Mental & emotional

Promotes healing, and feelings of serenity.

Increases love.

Spiritual

Promotes unconditional love.

Aids spiritual alignment.

Increases empathy & compassion.

Blue

Physical

Calms nervous system, lowering blood pressure and heart rate.

Reduces inflammation & fever. Supports weight loss.

Mental & emotional

Calms anger, restlessness & irritability.

Improves communication and promotes self-expression.

Increases honesty, loyalty & trust.

Spiritual

Promotes authenticity.

Brings about tranquility.

Indigo

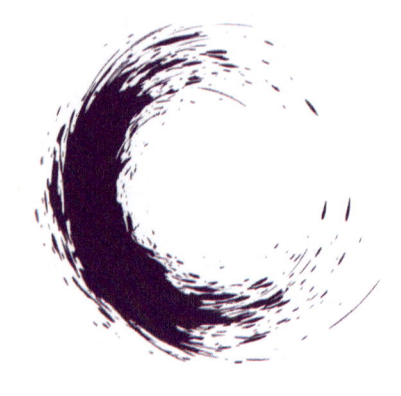

Physical

Heals ears, eyes & sinuses.

Relieves tension headaches & migraines.

Enhances immunity.

Mental & emotional

Promotes acceptance.

Aids clear thinking & decision making.

Broadens perspective.

Spiritual

Connects to intuition & spiritual guidance.

Purple

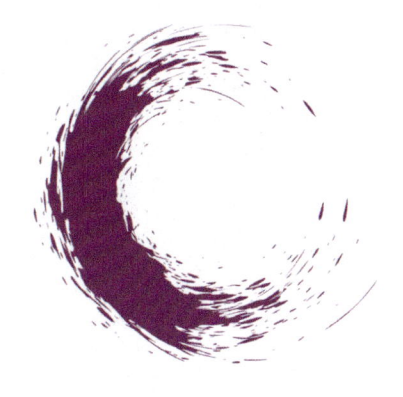

Physical

Promotes relaxation & aids sleep.

Reduces stress.

Boosts immune system.

Mental & emotional

Relaxing.

Supports meditation.

Brings about transformation.

Spiritual

Enhances spirituality.

Increases psychic awareness & abilities.

White

Physical

Cleanses & purifies.

Mental & emotional

Reduces negativity.

Boosts productivity.

Helps to resolve conflict.

Spiritual

Connects to higher self & consciousness.

Brings peace.

Black

Physical

Decreases energy.

Mental & emotional

Supports breaking bad habits, increases self-control.

Promotes independence.

Conveys authority.

Spiritual

Symbolises death, rebirth

and regeneration.

Brown

Physical

Aids hypertension.

Soothes hyperactivity.

Mental & emotional

Grounding.

Supports tradition & practicality.

Promotes comfort, stability & reliability.

Spiritual

Connects to Mother Earth.

Aids humility.

Grey

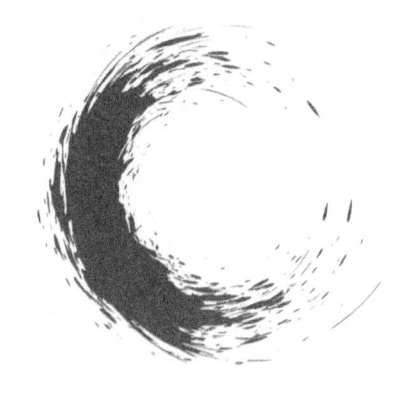

Physical

Decreases energy.

Mental & emotional

Promotes neutrality & compromise.

Increases depression.

Spiritual

Signifies a stalemate,

where nothing grows or recedes.

Gold

Physical

Increases energy.

Mental & emotional

Increases willpower & determination.

Spiritual

Promotes & enhances spirituality and leadership.

Connects to higher self and soul purpose.

Increases wisdom.

Silver

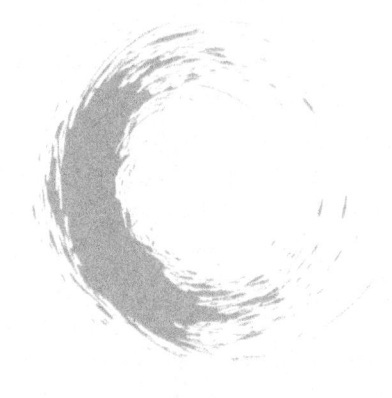

Physical

Soothes pain.

Mental & emotional

Enhances strategic thinking & brings clarity.

Assists reflection & contemplation.

Spiritual

Strengthens connections.

Promotes success.

Positivity in practice

Get colourful

Choose a colour (or two) to work with for a specific purpose, using the guide above if necessary, and begin to incorporate it into your surroundings via your wardrobe, interiors, and food. Dedicate some time to work with your chosen colour; it could be a day, a week, or a month. You might prefer to work intuitively and just 'know' when to switch to a different colour, or palette.

Try colur collecting

Spend some time collecting items of a chosen colour, or a rainbow of colours, from around your home and arrange them in any way you like. Take a photo of your collection and notice how you feel after the activity. Maybe even share it on your social media!

Get creative

Select a colourful creative project and have fun with it. This could be drawing, painting, sewing, flower arranging… anything of your choosing, just make it as colourful as possible.

Explore the chakras

Research what the 7 main chakras are, how they relate to the human body and how they are associated with the colours of the rainbow.

Layer on

"Colour" doesn't have to be a stand-alone positivity practice, you can use it to enhance any of the other positivity practices in this book, or any other practices that you have in your wellbeing toolkit. Explore how you can add a layer of colour to other areas of your life, such as using green when practising gratitude or pink when practising self love.

Affirmation

One of my favourite, and most frequently used Positivity Practices, affirmations are an absolute power tool for the mind. So very quick and easy to use, and yet they have such a BIG impact. I personally use them every day! So, what are they? Positive affirmations are, quite simply, uplifting phrases which we repeat to ourselves either out loud or quietly within our own mind. When used regularly, and repeatedly, they create a ripple effect that has the potential to bring about huge and powerful transformation - especially for our mental health and wellbeing.

The great thing about affirmations is that they are entirely mobile, meaning we can take them with us wherever we go. We can use them while we work, rest, exercise, meditate, play and even during sleep! Thinking them, and reciting them out loud are both very beneficial, but we can take it a step further by writing them down, in order to use as a visual reminder or by listening to them while we sleep. There are many free online recordings available across many different platforms, which we can listen to at any time.

So how do positive affirmations work? The mind is unable to differentiate between reality and fantasy - it will literally believe anything we tell it and then the physical body will respond accordingly. This is why it's so important to become aware of our thoughts – if we constantly tell ourselves that we are tired or worried, our brain will compute this to our mind and the body will begin to feel even more tired or anxious. By choosing to flip the narrative to the opposite kind of thoughts, we can make beneficial changes. For example, telling ourselves that we are energised instead of tired can help us to feel like we have more energy, because the body will believe it. By telling ourselves that we are calm instead of anxious, we can help to calm the nervous system and reduce tension in our body, making us feel calmer.

Sounds easy, right? Well, it is! The hardest part is remembering to practice them in the first place. Repetition is the key to success here, because the more we repeat our chosen affirmations, the deeper they are planted into our subconscious mind. Using them daily and turning them in to a healthy habit, is one of the best things we can do for our mental health.

Affirmations have been proven to be effective in several scientific studies; regularly repeating them has been shown to work on a cellular level, literally rewiring the neurological pathways of the brain for the better. The positive thoughts become embedded within the subconscious mind on a deep level, and that's how we begin to see changes in the way we think and, more importantly, in the way that we behave. Essentially, it's like tricking ourselves into healthier habits, in a really good way.

I first discovered affirmation when I was looking for natural and holistic ways to help myself overcome panic attacks and anxiety. At the time I felt so desperate that I was willing to try anything (except pharmaceuticals) and I'm glad I did because I now use them for all sorts of things, while my days of debilitating panic attacks are a distant memory. I began by creating colourful postcards with written affirmations on and leaving them on my dining table so that I could see them, encouraging me to recite them every morning during breakfast - a healthy habit that I still practice to this day. I also write a new affirmation each month on a chalk board in my kitchen. This helps me to stay accountable when daily life is busy, and I get distracted or forgetful. As well as visual reminders, I often start or finish my day by listening to guided affirmation practices on the Insight Timer app. The good thing about listening to affirmations is that the subconscious mind is always receptive, even when the conscious mind is busy - so you can conveniently listen to them while doing your hair before work, pottering about the house or whilst falling asleep... all that good stuff goes into the mind even when you don't realise it, and you get to reap the rewards later on.

The list of benefits of using positive affirmations is long and varied, among them are increased motivation and inspiration, which helps us to achieve our goals. Affirmations also help us to cultivate healthier habits, promoting healing and fostering a more balanced lifestyle. They can help us to change limiting beliefs, reduce anxiety and self-doubt, improve self-worth and self-esteem, and build confidence. They generally promote a more positive outlook on life and can help us shift our perspective. They also help to improve our relationship with ourselves and other people.

Affirmations work best when they are spoken in the present tense, and as if the desired outcome has already been achieved. For example, if we want to feel more confident, we can affirm the words "I am confident". This instantly creates that reaction within the mind and body and confidence begins to grow. The Law of Attraction dictates that the energy of those spoken words or thoughts will also attract more of the desired outcome. Whereas if we used the words "I want to be more confident", we'd be signalling to ourselves that we lack confidence and that's the energy we'd be putting out in to the world, and consequently attract back.

Using the words "I AM" at the beginning of any positive affirmation, is the most powerful way to work with them. Some other examples include;

I am courageous
I am calm
I am joyful
I am content
I am enough

Using visualisation to enhance your affirmation practice.

Affirmations are highly effective on their own, but there is a way to increase their value and make them even more beneficial; by combining them with the power of visualisation. When we focus the mind on what it would look like and, more importantly, *feel* like to have achieved our desired outcome, we create a ripple effect of positive energy that sets in motion a wave of change and transformation. When using the affirmation "I am confident", we can think or say the words whilst actually visualising how it feels to already be a highly confident person. Picturing confidence clearly in our minds, imagining how it feels, and being grateful for it, will send a clear signal to the parts of our brain which will make positive changes happen.

When used together, affirmations and visualisation are much more likely to create success in anything we do, whether it's achieving life-goals or improving our health, well-being and mindset.

As mentioned previously, when it comes to self-love/self-talk, the words we speak to ourselves have a huge impact on our mind and body so it's important to become aware of our thoughts and to consciously choose to uplift our mood and improve our mindset with positive phrases. This positivity practice can help us become happier, healthier, and even more abundant.

Affirmations have the power to transform all areas of our life, so I invite you to use them daily and watch as amazing shifts begin to happen.

Positivity in practice

Write or adopt a positive affirmation

Choose something which supports your currents needs. Display it in your home, workspace or on your electronic devices. Say it out loud or in your own mind, as many times as makes you feel good.

Supercharge your Vision Board

If you have one, add at least one positive affirmation to your Vision Board.

Switch it up

Change your affirmation from time to time, such as weekly or monthly.

Listen to a guide affirmation meditation online

Focus on the feeling behind each affirmation as you listen to the words. Visualise it as much as possible and express your gratitude for it as the meditation ends.

Meditation

Try a range of practices that benefit mind, body & soul

Meditation is my 'must have' when it comes to daily well-being practices, even if it's only for 5-10 minutes per day. Offering a huge range of benefits for the mind, body, heart, and soul, with zero negative side-effects, this really is a magnificent positivity practice!

In recent times, meditation, and mindfulness in particular, has become increasingly popular within the western world, but it is an ancient practice that has always been widely taught in the East. Our ancestors across the world knew how to meditate and understood why it's so good for us. It pleases me to see that it is now more accessible than ever and trying it for ourselves is as easy as picking up a phone, connecting to the internet and selecting a guided meditation. There's a variety of platforms available, many of which are free and offer a vast range of practices.

For those who are thinking of trying meditation for the first time, it can seem daunting because many people think that they can't meditate, or that they're required to sit in an uncomfortable, cross-legged position for an hour every day - which is not true, by the way. These are false assumptions which I am more than happy to dispel.

Anyone can meditate!

We don't have to stop thinking altogether nor do we have to 'empty the mind' - that really isn't the goal. Rather, we aim to give ourselves the time and space to just *be*, observing the thoughts that naturally arise, allowing them to come and go without judging them or interacting with them in any way.

Meditation has a calming effect on the nervous system, which is where relaxation inducing and stress reducing benefits for the body can begin to take place. Meditation is known to boost the immune system, as well as reduce symptoms of pain and inflammation within the body, offering relief for sufferers of conditions which can include; rheumatoid arthritis, asthma, fibromyalgia, and irritable bowel syndrome.

For the mind, mental health benefits include becoming less reactive to stressful situations, thinking more clearly, and improved memory, concentration, and cognitive function. Aside from meditation often being a peaceful experience, many creative ideas and insights can come from these moments of quiet solitude and stillness.

The 'monkey mind' is a concept that likens the mind to a wild monkey; in the same way that a monkey bounces around from one tree to the next to the next, in a fast-paced fashion, the untrained human mind can race around, jumping from one thought to another. The good news is that the mind can be trained, and our thoughts can be controlled. It just takes a little patience, practise, and perseverance.

On an emotional level, meditation can help us to become more self-aware and to build emotional resilience. It can also be very healing, empowering, confidence-boosting and can improve our self-esteem. I find it very comforting in times of stress and I've been using it for many years as a tool to help cope with anxiety.

One of my favourite things about meditation is that it brings us a sense of connection to our spirituality. It enables us to get in touch with our higher self, also known as our spirit or soul. We are, after all, loving souls having a human experience and it's so easy to forget this as we become consumed by our busy human lives. Many people experience spiritual awakenings through meditation practices, and some are even able to recall past life experiences! It's a practice which enables us to connect to our intuition - an inner knowing - often said to come from our higher self which can guide us through all aspects of life.

With so many styles to try and online teachers to guide us, we can really have fun exploring meditation. I invite you to think of it as an adventure, perhaps one that will become a life-long journey. Meditation is a practice, not a perfection, and it can sometimes require patience and self-compassion - being gentle on ourselves is a wise approach. Like anything, the more we practice the easier it becomes. Each session will provide a different experience depending on how our day is going and how we're feeling in any given moment.

The greatest rewards often come when our meditation practice is consistent and is carried out without judgement or expectation. Taking some time to try a variety of different types of meditation is worthwhile, because we are all different and what suits one person may not resonate with another. It is for us as individuals to explore what feels good and right for us, and in our own time too.

Brief guide to meditation styles

Guided

We listen to the voice of a teacher or guide, focusing our mind on the words they speak, and any images they suggest. Can also be used with visualisations to guide us into states of deep relaxation.

Visualisation

Where we focus the mind on visualising a specific image, and sometimes a feeling. It can also help us achieve our goals by envisioning the results of a desired outcome, as if they've already happened.

Concentration

Where we focus our attention on one particular thing, which could be an object or an image. This type of meditation can be done with the eyes open, such as gazing at a candle.

Mindfulness

The practice of bringing our awareness to the present moment, rather than engaging in thinking of past memories or future thoughts. Focusing on our five external senses of sight, sounds, smell, taste, and touch senses is a big part of mindfulness practices, as is simply observing our internal thoughts and emotions, without judgement.

Breath work/Pranayama

Prana = life force, Yama = control, therefore Pranayama means to control the breath. It's often used as tool to focus the mind and is a powerful tool to shift the body's state in times of stress. It is often used as a prelude to a deeper meditation practice.

Mantra

The repetition of a chosen sound or phrase, such as a mantra or affirmation is a form of concentration meditation. The practice focuses the mind fully on the one thing, allowing a time out from other thoughts and worries.

Transcendental

The aim is to calm the mind, slowing down and reducing thoughts, and then slipping into a state where thinking itself ceases to happen. Simply being, in a state of bliss, is attained.

Devotion

Used in various forms, across many different religions, the practice of devotion meditation can be used as a way of prayer or practicing dedication to God, during which the meditator focuses their minds on their chosen subject

Mindfulness

With our increasingly busy and active lifestyles, our minds have become more cluttered than ever. According to a study by the Laboratory of Neuro Imaging at the University of Southern California, the average person has about 48.6 thoughts per minute- that's up to 70,000 thoughts per day! Can you imagine how much more that would be for someone who is an over-thinker!

Worrying and stressing can become overwhelming for both the body and the mind; our thoughts often naturally wander from the present, to memories of the past and in to thoughts of the future. When we are highly anxious, it's common for the mind to negatively imagine or anticipate future events, most of which will never actually happen. When suffering from depression, the mind will frequently dwell too much on negative events or sad memories from the past.

Mindfulness sounds like a modern concept, but it is in fact an ancient form of meditation that has roots in Buddhism. It is the practice of focusing the mind on the present moment, observing things as they are without trying to change or control anything. It is one of the easiest forms of meditation to learn and for anyone looking to begin, this type of practice is a fantastic place to start!

When we focus on the present, stress and anxiety are reduced. There are many other benefits to mindfulness including finding equanimity and improved self-control. Mindfulness improves our attention span and ability to concentrate, as well as increasing our self-awareness.

Mindfulness enables us to take a step back and to respond to situations more wisely, rather than impulsively reacting to them. It can help with our ability to process emotions and to heal from traumatic experiences.

When we allow ourselves to acknowledge and feel emotions such as fear or anger, rather than resisting them, it helps to dissipate them. Mindfulness is a great tool for grounding and relieving the intensity of uncomfortable emotions, bringing rapid calm and clarity of mind. It also naturally cultivates self-acceptance, helping us to become more compassionate towards ourselves and others. It can be surprisingly good fun too, especially when practiced in groups! Many mindfulness tasks can trigger feelings of enjoyment, recollections of happy memories, and foster feelings of satisfaction.

So, whether you already have a regular meditation practice or you're a complete beginner, I invite you to try it out and perhaps add this powerful practice to your regular positivity toolkit. It can be used as a stand-alone practice, or it can be incorporated into other positivity practices such as self-love, setting boundaries, and releasing.

Take a mindful moment right now...

Positivity in practice

Pause reading this and take a look around you.

    Notice 5 things you can see.
    Listen for 4 things you can hear.
    Touch 3 things that you can feel.
    Try to notice 2 things you can smell.
    Notice 1 thing you can taste.

    Now, take a brief moment to notice how you feel…

    Well done!

Use a meditation app

If you don't already use one, explore what's available online and download one to try; I recommend 'Insight Timer' which is available for most smartphones. If you already use one, select a new or different mediation to your usual choice and give it a try. YouTube is also a great source of free online meditations.

Meditate within a group

Perhaps try a mediation or relaxation class or join an online group event. Practicing with others is supportive, encouraging and enhances the benefits.

Make it a regular thing

Explore the option of making meditation a regular practice. Be realistic with your goals and set aside some dedicated time for yourself to participate, even if it's for 5-10mins.

Release

Let go of anything which no longer serves you

Release, let go and forgive. Holding on to hurt, resentment, and negative thinking patterns will only weigh us down. By finding healing ways to let go of what no longer serves us we can liberate ourselves to move forward with a joyful heart and a newfound sense of freedom.

Release is quite possibly the most challenging of my positivity practices, while at the same time being one of the most beneficial. It can be highly transformational and liberating, and with it comes emotional freedom and a sense of peace. It also helps to reduce physical tension, allowing us to release tight and achy muscles.

Sometimes this practice requires courage and I think it's best done in a quiet space which is free from distraction and where you feel safe and free to unleash whatever wants to come out. It's also not a one-off practice, it's worth doing continuously and consistently, like watching the story of a book unfold one chapter at a time. To get the most value out of it, I would recommend setting aside a regular time and dedicate yourself to it. I personally practice this in alignment with the natural rhythms of the lunar cycles, sometimes alone and sometimes with a trusted friend or two. New moons and full moons are excellent times to practise this kind of healing work.

Imagine walking around carrying a heavy basket of shopping; the more you keep putting in the basket, the heavier it becomes. At some point, if you continue to keep adding to it without emptying something out first, the contents will either begin to overflow and spill out, or the basket will buckle under the strain. The mind works in much the same way, and we need to become aware of not letting it get overloaded in order to prevent mental and emotional burn out. There's only so much emotional heavyweight that we can carry before we become overwhelmed and inevitably crack under the pressure.

It's a healthy and healing practice to find ways to release pent-up emotions and tension. From a young age, we are strongly influenced by social conditioning and we are pressured by society's expectations, some of which are not right for us as individuals and can be unhealthy for us. By releasing and letting go of things like hurt and trauma, negative thinking and unhealthy behavioural patterns, we can help to bring balance to the mind and body, enabling ourselves to create space for more positive things such as clearer thinking, better decision making and the healthy processing of emotions. We increase our self-awareness and open up the pathway for personal and spiritual growth, which not only makes us happier and healthier as individuals, but also within our relationships.

The more of us who practice our ability to let go and release, the more we can positively influence others and help them to heal too. We can look to nature as a great example of this, by observing the trees outside. They instinctively know when autumn comes that they need to let their leaves die off and be released, and to pause in hibernation throughout winter, creating space for new growth in spring and the opportunity to bloom in summer. They don't struggle with it or resist the change of seasons, they simply accept it and allow what needs to be let go of to be released.

As discussed earlier, unprocessed emotions can get stuck in our physical bodies, causing tension and fatigue. Exercising is a great way to help release them and free the body from the harm that stress can cause, but what about the mind? How can we release mental stress? I have a few ways that I can recommend to help achieve this.

Meditation is a great tool to help us calm the mind, find clarity, and reduce confusion. It also helps us to connect to our intuition. It helps us to focus and identify what it is that needs to be released from our subconscious mind - the place we often unknowingly, store or hide away our feelings and emotions. Meditation can be used as a prelude to other releasing practises or used on its own. Guided meditations and visualisations are a supportive way to journey through a healing/releasing session and are an excellent technique for beginners. Other methods, such as concentration meditation, can set us up to release in other ways such as through the practice of journaling.

It's often said that a problem shared is a problem halved, and ain't that the truth! Sometimes, something as simple as just having a chat or a good rant to a trusted friend is all it takes to prevent us from bottling things up.

Some people don't know how to articulate their words or struggle to talk about their feelings, and so writing things down can be a great way to release them. Journaling is a more private method and a cathartic practice which enables us to express ourselves and process our thoughts and emotions.

After my dad died, I didn't know how to process or express my grief, so I bottled it up for a few years. I put on a brave face for the outside world and pretended that I was ok, but really I was feeling overwhelmed and lost inside. I remember living my life on autopilot, and feeling like I was watching myself move through life instead of actually living it.

I eventually reached a point where I knew I couldn't carry on like that and I desperately wanted to release the heavy weight of it, but I didn't quite know how. Then one day, after I'd finished college, I became acquainted with someone through work who it turns out lived next door to an old friend of mine with whom I had lost touch. We had been best friends throughout middle school, and she was a lovely friend, but I had unfairly distanced myself from her after my dad died. I had found it too painful to be around people who had known him and so had sought out new friends who didn't know the version of me that had existed before his passing. It was easier that way to hide my pain and to pretend it didn't exist. I'd often thought about her, missed her, and regretted my actions. These were the days before mobile phones and internet, so it was easier to lose touch with people. We had both moved house by then too, so any phone numbers we had for each other were no longer of any use. I saw this chance meeting with her neighbour as an opportunity to reconnect and apologise. Knowing that it would be impossible to say everything I wanted to say to her, face to face, I set about writing her a letter.

This was a real breakthrough in my healing journey, as well as being my chance to explain myself and offer the apology that she deserved. I spent a couple of hours writing that letter, pouring my heart out and shedding so many tears that had for so long not known how to come out. It was both painful and therapeutic, exhausting and at the same time extremely liberating! I found it so helpful in fact, that after I finished, I set about writing another letter - this one to my dad. I knew that it could never be sent, or read in any physical way, but deep down I believed in my heart that his spirit would be able to see or feel its contents. I wrote down everything, all that I wished I could have said to him and more. I really began to open my wounds that night and started to truly begin to process my grief. Knowing I couldn't send my dad's letter, and not wanting anyone else to read it, I chose to lovingly destroy it by burning it in the fire - I felt that having written it was enough, and that he would have somehow been able to read it if I released it out into the cosmos. This is a transformational healing technique which I still use today; sometimes I journal away the thoughts, feelings, and emotions which no longer serve me, and then I safely burn them with the intention of letting them go. It works really well!

Fortunately for me, my old friend received the letter, and she took the time to read it. She then got in touch, accepted my apology, and asked if we could meet up. She was kind and it was so good to see her! We even ended up working together for a short time before I moved away. She doesn't know it, but she showed me the power of forgiveness. After she forgave me, I then decided it was time for me to forgive myself which ultimately helped me to lovingly accept my loss, let go of my grief and to move forward with a different outlook on life.

One of the reasons I'm "so positive" is because I believe that the best way to honour someone's memory is to live life to the fullest. It doesn't mean we'll ever forget them or lose the love we shared, but we can appreciate the life we have now and the people with whom we share it, by experiencing joy and love. We all have the strength within us to overcome challenges and obstacles, to let go, and to release, forgive, and heal.

Other techniques for releasing emotions can include expressing ourselves through art, music, dance, or creative writing such as poetry. Sometimes we may need to seek help from a professional therapist or healer for more serious issues or simply to have the reassurance and support of a qualified practitioner. Hypnotherapy, counselling, and ha'oponono (the ancient Hawaiian practice of forgiveness) are very beneficial. Holistic and complementary therapies such acupuncture and massage are also options worth considering.

Whichever method we choose, releasing emotional stress can be painful, uncomfortable, and often a little bit scary. I advise you to be patient with, and compassionate towards yourself. Even now I often cry when I practice letting go, but that's okay because I understand that tears are not a bad thing - tears are healing and to let them flow is a natural emotional release. That old saying "it's better out than in" comes to mind, and for me it's certainly applicable. It feels like such a relief after.

This practice works in much the same way insofar as after a good cry we often feel drained and tired, tending to sleep more heavily and then wake up the next day feeling lighter. Sometimes mild symptoms of a 'healing crisis' can occur, which can include; headaches, weariness, sensitivity to sound and light, dizziness, sweating, bodily aches, or even nausea. This is all good and temporary though - it simply means that the body is releasing its toxins! I find it helpful to drink plenty of water before, during, and after, and to follow up with a good cleanse by means of a shower or salt bath. We could even consider it an act of self-care and approach it as a little bit of well-deserved pampering.

All of this is much easier said than done, but looking at it from the perspective of how it feels afterwards, we are able to look back and feel glad that we have put the work in. I classify this as a restorative practice and I come through the other side of it feeling transformed and restored mentally, emotionally, physically, and spiritually.

The effort is worth it. The rewards are worth it. YOU are worth it.

Releasing enables us to learn from our experiences, and if we can embrace the lessons we learn along the way with a grateful heart, we move forward having gained personal and spiritual growth, wisdom, and insight. It provides us with the opportunity to move forward and to enjoy life in a lighter, more positive way.

Take some time to reflect.

Positivity in practice

Find Solitude

Spend a bit of time in solitude for contemplation, without distractions, and allow yourself to think about and feel whatever is arising within you. Then decide how it would suit you best to release it…

Journal it out

Write down anything that needs to come out. It could be thoughts and feelings, or a letter that which will never be sent. The purpose here is to no longer hold it in, to express it outwardly. You have the option to destroy the letter afterwards.

Feel the burn

Sometimes (safely) burning what you've written is a great way to let go and release. Use your fireplace, or a fireproof container to set it alight and be sure to dispose of the ashes in a safe manner.

Sweat it out

Exercising is a great way to release emotions, especially if you're angry. Try something cardio based, such as boxing to blow off steam.

Share or offload it

Call, text or go visit a friend. Ask if you can chat, rant, vent, or cry! Sometimes you just need someone to listen, even if you don't wish to discuss it further or find a solution. A good friend will simply let you offload.

Ask for help

If there's a more serious issue that you're struggling with, or feel you can't discuss with friends or family, don't be afraid to ask for help from someone else. Your doctor or health centres are there to help, as are voluntary organisations such as The Samaritans.

Finding Joy

Look for & appreciate all the joy in your life

All thoughts and feelings emit an energetic frequency which can be measured in hertz. The emotional vibrational scale shows us the range of emotions and their frequencies in two ranges: positive, and negative.

Joy is shown to be a high vibrational emotion. I mean, who doesn't like feeling joyful? It's fantastic! Just for fun, let me share with you that joy resonates at a frequency of 540hz. For the sake of comparison, here are some examples of lower vibrational emotions: shame sits at 20hz and anger at 150hz. So, when we talk about 'raising our vibrations' or uplifting our mood, we mean it literally! Other high vibrational emotions include love at 500hz, and peace at 600hz- It's interesting to note here, that joy actually has a higher frequency than love.

Why do we want to aim for high vibrational emotions? Quite simply because they have a positive impact on our well-being. They produce feel good hormones which result in us becoming happier and healthier. Negative, low vibrational emotions trigger the body's stress response, dragging us down both physically and mentally.

Our physiology changes when we worry, feel stressed, and are unhappy; the body will begin to hunch or slouch, because we are biologically and ancestrally programmed to withdraw into a foetal position when we feel threatened. Lower vibrational emotions, such as anger and fear, lead to shallow breathing and tense muscles. Notice how we frown when we are irritated or grit our teeth if we feel frustrated or angry. Our temperature rises (along with our heart rate and blood pressure).

With this in mind, it's important to become aware of the quality of our thoughts and to consciously choose what emotions we give our energy to. After all, energy flows where focus goes!

The good news is that we have the power to control this at will. I don't think I know of anyone who would choose unhappiness over happiness. Have you noticed that you can instantaneously burst into a smile the moment we think of a happy memory? Or burst out laughing when you recall a funny moment?

These are thoughts that create positive reactions within our bodies; on a physical level it can actually help to lessen pain, boost the immune system, and improve our sleep. Laughter increases our oxygen levels, nourishing the blood and all the organs and tissues of our body. Happy thoughts leave us feeling lighter and more relaxed. When we feel happy we stand taller, our eyes open wider and sparkle more. Joy is an emotion which increases feelings of satisfaction, it elevates our confidence and boosts self-esteem. It's also positively contagious; when other people see and feel our joy, it makes them feel joyful too.

While it's not possible to completely avoid stressful people, places, or circumstances, we can choose to limit the time we spend around them. We can also control the amount of time and energy that we direct towards negative thinking. We can reroute those thoughts and reframe our minds by focusing on, and striving for, higher vibrational emotions.

I invite you to spend some time reflecting on who, where, and what brings you joy? Who/what uplifts you? What do you enjoy doing? Where are the happy places that you enjoy being? Who makes you laugh or smile? Who are the people whose company you enjoy being around? Invest more time and energy on these people, places, and things and notice the positive effect they have on you.

On a personal level, I love to focus on joy. After having come through the worst years of my life, experiencing the sadness and grief that I felt when my dad passed away, I decided that life really is worth living. I think the best way to honour someone's memory is to live life to its fullest, and to fill it with as much joy as we possibly can.

I love creative projects. It makes me really happy to hand craft my Christmas cards. I love the festive season, especially the colourful decorations, jolly music, and the feeling of excitement that fills the air. All year round I love to walk my dog, read books, and have long soaks in the bath. I love yoga and meditation, and teaching them brings me so much more joy. I'm incredibly grateful to have created The Positivity Project; hosting the social media projects was so much fun! I also found them to be very inspiring (hence the writing of this book) as well as unexpectedly boosting my own confidence, sense of purpose, and self-worth, in the process.

Reflecting upon and focusing on joy is a practice which I recommend repeating on a regular basis. Doing so reinforces the benefits, and keeps the intention behind it at the forefront of our minds. Not only is this a benefit to us and our own well-being, but it's also good for the people around us too because like attracts like. Our joyful energy can be seen, felt, and shared, uplifting both ourselves and others. It improves the relationships in our lives and often inspires other people, so go ahead and lead by example - put a smile on your face, spread your wings, and become a powerhouse of positivity by choosing to radiate joy.

Reflect on the joy in your life.

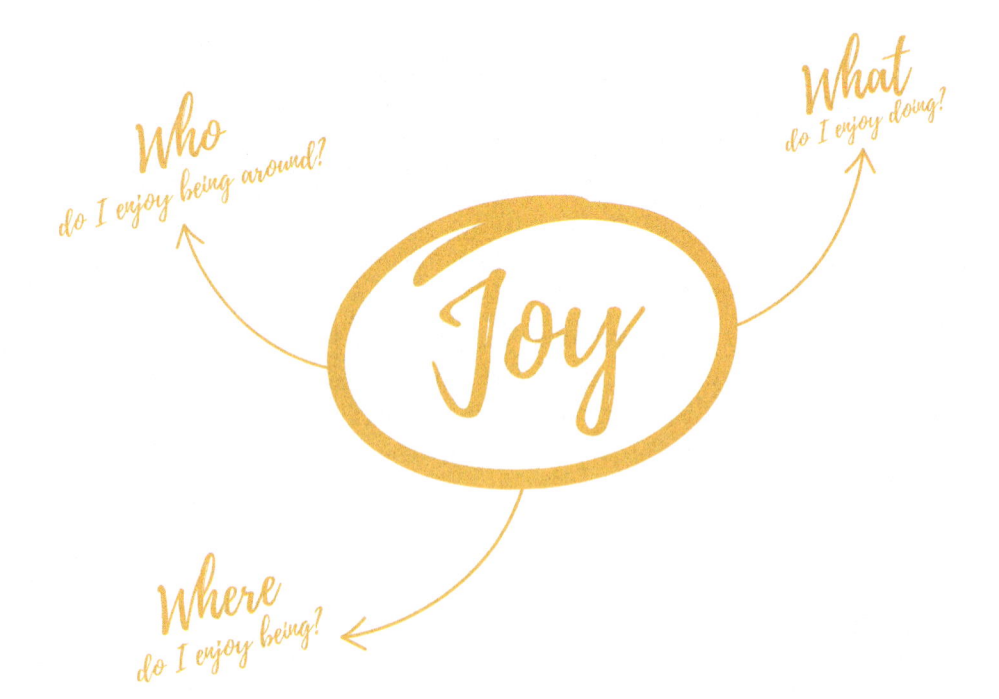

Who do I enjoy being around?

What do I enjoy doing?

Joy

Where do I enjoy being?

Positivity in practice

Make a list, or draw a spider diagram which sets out all of the sources of joy in your life. Include people, pets, places, and activities. Leave it somewhere visible for at a least a week to remind you of, and to appreciate them all.

Spend more time doing joyful things

Referring to your list or diagram, make a conscious choice to spend more time with the people who bring you joy, and participating in the things that make you feel happy.

Watch a comedy

Be it a movie, a show or a live performance. Spend some time watching some kind of comedy that makes you laugh.

Recall a funny memory

Think of a time when something or someone made you belly laugh. Really recall that memory in as much detail as possible and focus on it for a few minutes. Notice what happens to your body and your mood.

Be the joy in someone else's day

Do something for someone else, that will make them smile or laugh. Spread the joy around!

Use the colour orange to enhance or bring more joy in to your life.

The Emotional Vibrational Scale

Joy 540 hz

Peace 600 hz

Love 500 hz

Reason 400 hz

Acceptance 350 hz

Willingness 310 hz

Neutrality 250 hz

Courage 200 hz

Pride 175 hz

Anger 150 hz

Desire 125 hz

Fear 100 hz

Grief 75 hz

Despair 50 hz

Guilt 30 hz

Shame 20 hz

Play!

Embrace your inner child and feel free!

How old are you? Does it matter? Your age describes your body, not your spirit. We all have to be responsible adults when we need to be, but what about those precious moments when we don't...?

Life doesn't have to be all work, chores, and to-do lists. For my final positivity practice, I invite you to embrace your inner child with me; I invite you to go out (or stay in) and Play!

No matter how old we are, 'play time' allows positive energy to flow within and all around us. When we play, we embody joy, uplifting ourselves and those around us. Often, it's the simple things that we find the most fun, creative, and carefree. These are the things which connect us to our inner child, allowing us to feel liberated from negative thinking and the restrictions of our minds. How long has it been since you splashed in puddles, climbed a tree, or kicked your feet through piles of leaves? When did you last skip along a path, laugh at stupid jokes with your friends, watched cartoons by yourself, or blew bubbles just for the fun of it? Spending time with the children, pets or 'kidults' in your life is helpful too - interact with them often. Join in with their playful activities and notice how it makes you feel.

If you're anything like me, you may have done some of those things earlier today! For others, you may have played fairly recently depending on what season it is. Thinking about these things literally makes me smile as I type these words, and I'm convinced they keep us youthful too. I've never had any children of my own, but being the big kid that I am, and always having had the presence of children in my life, I always manage to find time to get playful! At most of the gatherings with family and friends that I attend I can, more often than not, be found joining in games with the kids while the other adults drink alcohol and talk about grown up stuff in the other room. I love playing hide & seek, and I'm more than happy to embrace my inner child.

So, what is the inner child, as why is it so beneficial for us to connect with it?

The inner child is a subconscious part of us. The innocent part, often held within childhood memories which existed before life's experiences shaped the adults that we have become today. A part of it is the playful, imaginative, and hopeful dreamer that hasn't a care in the world. It is simply free and content to have fun.

The other aspect is the shadow of our childhood fears and worries, which often influences our future thinking habits and behavioural patterns. As we grow up, we naturally become disconnected and distant from our inner child as we take on social programming, and the busyness of life, along with its responsibilities and stresses. As grown-ups we still carry within us our childhood emotions, memories, and beliefs, as well as our hopes and dreams for the future.

Taking time to connect to our inner child is important. It's also beneficial in so many ways. As well as enabling us to heal any wounds from childhood trauma, which in itself is incredibly liberating, it reduces stress and anxiety. It can also help us to become more self-aware, compassionate, and more understanding of others. Like all of my other positivity practices, it has multiple physical health benefits too; the release of endorphins, improved memory and brain function, increased stamina, strength, balance, and fitness. The list goes on.
It's worth noting that, as well as seeking adventure and happiness, the inner child ultimately wants to feel safe and nurtured. When we pay attention to, and fulfil those needs, we can really raise our positivity mindset. Connecting to the inner child, for both healing and for engaging in playtime, can help us to find emotional freedom, build resilience, and discover courage that we didn't know we had. It increases our zest for life, inspiration, and vitality. It helps us to find satisfaction and contentment - how wonderful would it be to feel all of those things!

Often the simplicity of play time is most beneficial because as adults we tend to overthink and unnecessarily overcomplicate things. Play is a practice which is simple, mindful, joyful and in my opinion, truly beautiful.

I encourage you to carve out some time to get playful. When was the last time you coloured in a picture, or wrote a story? When did you last play a board game, swing on the swings in the park, or skip with a rope? I invite you to try some of these things, and more. Whether it's singing, dancing, laughing, or just being creative in some way, do whatever feels right and good for you.

Don't be self-conscious and don't hold back - see if you can wholeheartedly embrace the moment and notice how it makes you feel. You are never too old to enjoy life and it passes by so fast, which is why I positively encourage you to make the most of every opportunity to Play!

Positivity in practice

Go play

Choose one or more of the activities mentioned in this chapter and go do it!

Invite some friends

Arrange a play date or organise a games night with a mate or two and go have some fun!

Listen to your inner child

If you ask, your inner child will tell you what it needs. Whether it's healing, playtime, or anything else. Take some time to quietly look within and connect to your inner child (guided meditations for this specific purpose can be readily found online).

Create

There are plenty of suggestions in this chapter but remember that children (and kidults) like to create or invent their own games and activities!

Recreate

If you have a particular childhood memory that you're fond of, you could recreate it! If it's a place, go revisit it.
If it's an activity, recreate it.
If it's a game, play it!

Conclusion

Thank you for taking the time to read The Positivity Project, and well done if you have tried any of these positivity practices for yourself. Whilst your journey through The Positivity Project book now draws to a close, your own practises don't have to!

I invite you to carry forward any of the tools and techniques that I've shared and begin to layer them into your daily lives. What starts with a practice, can turn in to a healthy habit and if you allow it, can become a way of life.

Please remember that practice does not require perfection, and any kind of progress is a positive thing. I believe that every single one of us has the potential to be a powerhouse of positivity, and to contribute to making the world a better place. As we uplift ourselves, we uplift others. I encourage you to lead by example; be gentle on yourselves, be kind, be unique, and most of all, be grateful.

You are also welcome to join me and other followers on my social media platforms where you can find videos from the project, and invitations to try some positivity practises such as guided meditations, self love exercises and colour inspiration. It's also an opportunity to join in with our little community of like minded wellbeing warriors.

About the Author

Marie Parkinson is an holistic meditation & yoga teacher in County Durham, UK. For many years, Marie felt she had something more to offer the Universe, she felt a 'calling', or 'life purpose' was curled up inside her, just waiting to unfurl. Several years ago she made the conscious decision to accept these calls from the Universe and plunged herself right in. She offered herself open to opportunities to share her wealth of experience whilst continuing to enrich herself with all manner of learning from across the wellbeing and spiritual spectrum. Since then, Marie has flourished into what can only be described as an influential and spiritually conscious guide and mentor for individuals and groups, helping others to align with their own higher selves, teaching calmness and reflection through a portfolio of online projects, in-person workshops and classes, and now through her books.

Marie is passionate in immersing herself in the natural environment accompanied by her companion, Bramble, a loyal border terrier whose character outweighs her stature by an order of magnitude. She has a relentlessly playful attitude, and she lets this shine by spending lots of time with her family and friends.

You can find Marie online by searching for "Meditate with Marie" where you can contact her personally, and can enjoy soaking up some of her videos and written content which she has created and shared with her growing online community.

Printed in Great Britain
by Amazon